THE
BASEBALL
QUIZ
BOOK

THE BASEBALL QUIZ BOOK

TED MISA

HAWTHORN BOOKS, INC.
Publishers/New York

TO
DAD ("Chappie")—
A Bigger Sports Buff than I

Library of Congress Catalog Card Number: 74–339
ISBN: 0–8015–0524–0

  2 3 4 5 6 7 8 9 10

CONTENTS

1.

BASEBALL QUIZ — MULTIPLE CHOICE

1. Name the player who has won the MVP award in both the AL and NL?
   a. *Richie Allen*   b. *Amos Otis*   c. *Matty Alou*   d. *Frank Robinson*
2. Who was the last player to hit over .400?
   a. *Ty Cobb*   b. *Ted Williams*   c. *Ralph Kiner*   d. *Joe DiMaggio*
3. What was the batting average of the last player to hit over .400?
   a. *.406*   b. *.407*   c. *.411*   d. *.409*
4. Who holds the ML record for most stolen bases in 1 season?
   a. *Bert Campaneris*   b. *Ty Cobb*   c. *Maury Wills*   d. *Lou Brock*
5. What is the record for most stolen bases in 1 season?
   a. *96*   b. *100*   c. *111*   d. *104*
6. Who holds the record for most consecutive games played?
   a. *Billy Williams*   b. *Lou Gehrig*   c. *Ty Cobb*   d. *Willie Mays*
7. What is the record for most consecutive games played?
   a. *2,217*   b. *2,001*   c. *2,130*   d. *2,013*
8. Who holds the NL record for most home runs in a double header?
   a. *Johnny Mize*   b. *Stan Musial*   c. *Hank Aaron*   d. *Home Run Baker*

1

9. Who holds the record for most consecutive home runs in consecutive games?

    a. *Rudy York*   b. *Dale Long*   c. *Larry Doby*   d. *Walt Dropo*

10. Name the active pitcher with the most career home runs.

    a. *Vida Blue*   b. *Bob Gibson*   c. *Tom Seaver*   d. *Jim Hunter*

11. What is the most career home runs hit by a pitcher? Name him.

    a. *37*   b. *20*   c. *22*   d. *17*

12. How many times did Babe Ruth hit 4 home runs in a game?

    a. *3*   b. *1*   c. *0*   d. *7*

13. What is the most runs scored in an inning since 1900?

    a. *17*   b. *11*   c. *21*   d. *13*

14. What team scored the most runs in a half inning?

    a. *Yankees*   b. *Tigers*   c. *Red Sox*   d. *Dodgers*

15. Who was the youngest player to play for a ML team?

    a. *Hank Aaron*   b. *Willie Mays*   c. *Cy Young*   d. *Joe Nuxhall*

16. What was the original shape of home plate?

    a. *round*   b. *square*   c. *diamond*   d. *polygon*

17. Who was the youngest player elected to the Baseball Hall of Fame?

   a. *Roberto Clemente* b. *Sandy Koufax* c. *Lou Gehrig*
      d. *Christy Matthewson*

18. What was the distance of the longest home run ever hit?

   a. *600 ft.* b. *500 ft.* c. *565 ft.* d. *601 ft.*

19. Who holds the record for the longest consecutive game hitting streak?

   a. *Stan Musial* b. *Joe DiMaggio* c. *Ted Williams* d. *Pete Rose*

20. How many games did this consecutive hitting streak cover?

   a. *37* b. *45* c. *56* d. *28*

21. Name the 2 players who hit 2 grand slam home runs in 1 game other than Frank Robinson, who achieved this feat, June 26, 1970.

   a. *Mantle* b. *Ruth* c. *Northrup* d. *Stargell*
      Maris   *Gehrig*   *Gentile*   *Bonds*

22. Who holds the career record for stealing home the most times?

   a. *Maury Wills* b. *Jackie Robinson* c. *Ty Cobb* d. *Bert Campaneris*

23. What is the brand name of baseballs used in the ML?

   a. *Rawlings* b. *Wilson* c. *McGregor* d. *Spalding*

24. Which player has the highest lifetime batting average?

   a. *Honus Wagner* b. *Stan Musial* c. *Ty Cobb* d. *Ted Williams*

25. Name the ballpark where night baseball is not played?

   a. *Fenway Park*   b. *Wrigley Field*   c. *Jarry Park*
   d. *Memorial Stadium*

26. From what sport did baseball originate?

   a. *squash* b. *polo* c. *cricket* d. *handball*

27. What is the record for most hits in a 7-game WS?

   a. *13* b. *10* c. *11* d. *12*

28. Who pitched the only perfect WS game?

   a. *Cy Young* b. *Don Larsen* c. *Robin Roberts* d. *Sandy Koufax*

29. What year did Babe Ruth hit his 714th home run?

   a. *1934* b. *1932* c. *1935* d. *1937*

30. What team has won the most WS?

   a. *Giants* b. *Dodgers* c. *Yankees* d. *Athletics*

31. What is the distance of the base lines?

   a. *60 ft.*   b. *90 ft.*   c. *75 ft.*   d. *65 ft.*

32. Who holds the ML record for most home runs in a season?

   a. *Babe Ruth*   b. *Hank Greenberg*   c. *Roger Maris*
   d. *Hack Wilson*

33. Name the pitcher who struck out 15 batters in his first ML appearance?

   a. *Sandy Koufax*   b. *Whitey Ford*   c. *Warren Spahn*
   d. *Bob Feller*

34. Who was the first black player to play in the ML?

   a. *Monte Irvin*   b. *Ernie Banks*   c. *Jackie Robinson*
   d. *Satchel Paige*

35. How many teams are there in the ML?

   a. *18*   b. *24*   c. *16*   d. *28*

36. How many umpires are there in a WS game?

   a. *6*   b. *4*   c. *8*   d. *7*

37. What player once played for the Harlem Globetrotters?

   a. *Vida Blue*   b. *Bob Gibson*   c. *Bobby Bonds*   d. *Ferguson Jenkins*

38. Who holds the record for most career grand slam home runs?

   a. *Ted Williams*   b. *Johnny Mize*   c. *Gil Hodges*   d. *Lou Gehrig*

39. Who holds the WS mark for most batters hit by a pitcher in 1 game?

   a. *Babe Ruth*   b. *Whitey Ford*   c. *Vic Raschi*   d. *Bruce Kison*

40. What team had 2 switch-hitting catchers at the same time?

   a. *Cardinals*   b. *Giants*   c. *Twins*   d. *Expo's*

41. Which player holds the record for most career pinch-hits?

   a. *Dusty Rhodes*   b. *Orlando Cepeda*   c. *Smokey Burgess*
   d. *Enos Slaughter*

42. Name the player who holds the record for most walks.

   a. *Lou Gehrig*   b. *Ty Cobb*   c. *Babe Ruth*   d. *Mel Ott*

43. Who holds the record for most times hit by a pitch?

   a. *Felix Millan*   b. *Phil Rizzuto*   c. *Pee Wee Reese*   d. *Ron Hunt*

44. In how many ML games did Walt Alston play?

   a. *51*   b. *150*   c. *1*   d. *24*

45. For what team did Walt Alston play?

   a. *Athletics*   b. *Browns*   c. *Dodgers*   d. *Cardinals*

46. When Don Larsen pitched his perfect game, who was his opponent?

   a. *Juan Marichal*   b. *Sal Maglie*   c. *Hoyt Wilhelm*   d. *Jim Hearn*

47. Which team first wore numbers on its uniforms?

    a. *Cardinals* b. *Tigers* c. *Red Sox* d. *Yankees*

48. What year were numbers first worn on baseball uniforms?

    a. *1921* b. *1929* c. *1924* d. *1931*

49. During Joe DiMaggio's 56-game hitting streak, how many home runs did he hit?

    a. *14* b. *0* c. *7* d. *15*

50. Which Twins player has led the AL in batting 3 times through 1972?

    a. *Harmon Killebrew* b. *Rod Carew* c. *Tony Oliva*
    d. *Bob Allison*

51. Who led the NL in doubles in 1958?

    a. *Eddie Mathews* b. *Orlando Cepeda* c. *Gil Hodges*
    d. *Rich Ashburn*

52. Who led the NL in total bases in 1971?

    a. *Joe Torre* b. *Lou Brock* c. *Pete Rose* d. *Joe Morgan*

53. Who was the first Met player to hit 3 home runs in 1 game?

    a. *Frank Thomas*   b. *Donn Clendennon*   c. *Marv
    Throneberry* d. *Jim Hickman*

54. Who is the only NL player to hit 2 grand slam home runs in 1 game?

    a. *Tony Cloninger*   b. *Ernie Banks*   c. *Nate Colbert*
    d. *Bobby Bonds*

55. Who was the last player to execute an unassisted triple play?

    a. *Lou Boudreau*   b. *Ron Hansen*   c. *Glenn Beckert*
    d. *Don Kessinger*

56. Which shortstop participated in the most double plays in 1 season?

    a. *Mark Belanger*   b. *Chris Spier*   c. *Bobby Wine*
    d. *Bud Harrelson*

57. How many home runs did Home Run Baker hit in his 13-year career?

    a. *93*   b. *150*   c. *490*   d. *260*

58. In what year did Babe Ruth hit 60 home runs?

    a. *1934*   b. *1927*   c. *1935*   d. *1924*

59. Who was the first catcher to win the MVP award 3 times?

    a. *Bill Dickey*   b. *Yogi Berra*   c. *Del Crandell*   d. *Mickey Cochran*

60. Who was the youngest player to hit his 100th career home run?

    a. *Tony Conigliaro*   b. *Ted Williams*   c. *Babe Ruth*
    d. *Willie Mays*

61. Who hit the first home run in Shea Stadium?

    a. *Frank Thomas*   b. *Willie Stargell*   c. *Billy Williams*
    d. *Willie Mays*

62. What is the ML record for most doubles by a batter in 1 game?

    a. *3*   b. *5*   c. *6*   d. *4*

63. In how many All-Star games did Ted Williams play?

    a. *19* b. *18* c. *11* d. *20*

64. How many players share the achievement of getting 6 straight hits in 1 game?

    a. *7* b. *14* c. *25* d. *37*

65. Which team used the most pitchers in a 9-inning game?

    a. *Indians* b. *Browns* c. *Braves* d. *Senators*

66. How many times did Ty Cobb steal home?

    a. *40* b. *19* c. *32* d. *27*

67. Who was the only pitcher ever to hit a grand slam home run in a WS game?

    a. *Bob Gibson* b. *Don Drysdale* c. *Dave McNally*
    d. *Juan Marichal*

68. Name the 2 teams that played a game in which a home run was hit in every inning.

    a. *Phillies* b. *Dodgers* c. *Cardinals* d. *Yankees*
    and *Pirates* and *Giants* and *Cubs* and *Red Sox*

69. Which NL player won the slugging title in 1973?

    a. *Hank Aaron* b. *Darrell Evans* c. *Nate Colbert*
    d. *Willie Stargell*

70. How many home runs did Hank Aaron, Darrell Evans, and Dave Johnson hit in 1973, combined?

   a. *100*   b. *124*   c. *112*   d. *99*

71. Who led the NL in strikeouts in October 1973?

   a. *Bobby Bonds*   b. *Ron Santo*   c. *Willie Stargell*
   d. *Tony Perez*

72. Who led the NL in 1973 in most bases on balls?

   a. *Pete Rose*   b. *Darrell Evans*   c. *Cleon Jones*   d. *Billy Williams*

73. Against whom did Harmon Killebrew hit home run number 500?

   a. *Ken Holtzman*   b. *Billy Hoeft*   c. *Vida Blue*   d. *Mike Cuellar*

74. To which team was Ralph Kiner of the Pirates traded in 1953?

   a. *Cubs*   b. *Mets*   c. *Braves*   d. *Reds*

75. Who in the AL ranks second on the all-time home run list?

   a. *Ted Williams*   b. *Frank Robinson*   c. *Mickey Mantle*
   d. *Jimmy Foxx*

76. Who holds the NL record for most stolen bases in a lifetime?

   a. *Maury Wills*   b. *Honus Wagner*   c. *Max Carey*
   d. *Jackie Robinson*

77. How many complete games did Steve Carlton pitch enroute to his 27–10 record in 1972?

   a. *30*   b. *12*   c. *19*   d. *31*

78. How many men were on base when Horace Clark hit his first 2 ML home runs?

   a. *0*   b. *1*   c. *2*   d. *3*

79. Which Met player won the WS MVP award in 1969?

   a. *Tommy Agee*   b. *Donn Clendennon*   c. *Tom Seaver*
   d. *Bud Harrelson*

80. How many career home runs did Ralph Houk have?

   a. *7*   b. *12*   c. *0*   d. *3*

81. Who was the first black coach in the AL?

   a. *Larry Doby*   b. *Elston Howard*   c. *Junior Gilliam*
   d. *Monte Irvin*

82. Who once hit 10 home runs in 20 at bats?

   a. *Roger Maris*   b. *Hank Aaron*   c. *Babe Ruth*   d. *Frank
   Howard*

83. Which pennant-winning team had the lowest won-and-lost
    percentage in ML history?

   a. *Mets*   b. *Cardinals*   c. *Cubs*   d. *Orioles*

84. Which NL team ended the 1973 season with the highest slug-
    ging percentage?

   a. *Reds*   b. *Braves*   c. *Giants*   d. *Padres*

85. Which NL team ended the 1973 season as the only team with
    a slugging percentage below .350?

   a. *Phillies*   b. *Padres*   c. *Expo's*   d. *Mets*

86. As of the end of the 1973 season, who is the only original
    player still with the Mets?

   a. *Cleon Jones*   b. *Jerry Grote*   c. *Tom Seaver*   d. *Ed
   Kranepool*

87. Who won the AL batting crown in 1973 with a .350 average?

 a. *George Scott*   b. *Bobby Murcer*   c. *Rod Carew*
 d. *Tommy Davis*

88. How many home runs did Reggie Jackson hit in 1973 to win the AL home run crown?

 a. *40*   b. *32*   c. *36*   d. *43*

89. How many total home runs were hit in the AL in 1973?

 a. *1,000*   b. *1,607*   c. *1,552*   d. *1,525*

90. Which AL team led the league in team batting in 1973 with a percentage of .273?

 a. *A's*   b. *Red Sox*   c. *Twins*   d. *Orioles*

91. Which AL team led all other teams in home runs in 1973 with a total of 158?

 a. *Yankees*   b. *Orioles*   c. *Twins*   d. *Indians*

92. Who led the Oakland A's in stolen bases in 1973 with 53?

 a. *Bert Campaneris*   b. *Bill North*   c. *Reggie Jackson*
 d. *Joe Rudi*

93. Who led the AL in most hits in 1973 with 203?

 a. *Rod Carew*   b. *Al Bumbry*   c. *George Scott*   d. *Bert Campaneris*

94. In 1973 Nolan Ryan set a new ML record for most strikeouts by a pitcher in 1 season. How many strikeouts did he get?

 a. *382*   b. *309*   c. *383*   d. *394*

95. How many times did Babe Ruth win the Baseball Writers Association MVP award?

a. *0* b. *2* c. *1* d. *3*

96. Who was the first ML player to be intentionally walked with the bases loaded?

a. *Nap Lajoie* b. *Babe Ruth* c. *Lou Gehrig* d. *Rogers Hornsby*

97. Who has pitched more ML games than anyone else?

a. *Cy Young* b. *Hoyt Wilhelm* c. *Satchel Paige* d. *Christy Matthewson*

98. Who was the only AL player to score more than 100 runs in 1972?

a. *Bobby Murcer* b. *Bert Campaneris* c. *Dick Allen* d. *John Mayberry*

2.

NICKNAMES

How many players, past and present, can you identify by their nicknames?

1.	Scooter	13.	Iron Horse
2.	Bambino	14.	Clipper
3.	Say Hey	15.	Fireball
4.	Moose	16.	Skoonj
5.	Catfish	17.	Pee Wee
6.	Roadrunner	18.	Hammer
7.	Snuffy	19.	Sultan of Swat
8.	Monster	20.	Tug
9.	Stick	21.	Casey
10.	Stretch	22.	Bobo
11.	Duke	23.	Fordham Flash
12.	Home Run	24.	Pistol

25. The Junkman

26. Yogi

27. Killer

28. Jumping Joe

29. Preacher

30. Chief

31. Stork

32. Vulture

33. Pepper

34. Hondo

35. Country

36. Granny

37. Boog

38. Dusty

39. Peanuts

40. High Pockets

41. Big Poison

42. Little Poison

43. Pie

44. Ducky

45. King Kong

46. Splendid Splinter

47. Hot Rod

48. Boomer

49. The Man

50. Blue Moon

51. Smokey

52. Old Eagle Eye

53. Schnozz

54. Little Napoleon

55. Frenchy

56. Squatty

57. Flash

58. Muggs

59. Augie

60. Spud

61. Bruno

62. Comet

63. Sudden Sam

64. Diamond Jim

65. Little Professor

66. Bo

67. Charlie Hustle

68. Sonny

69. Barber

70. Cap

71. Twinkle Toes

72. Heinie

73. Beetles

74. Goose

75. Cookie

76. Hoot

77. Cha-Cha

78. Shoeless Joe

79. Vinegar Bend

80. Klu

81. Uncle Robby

82. Newk

83. Prince Hal

84. Whip

85. Rabbit

86. Luke

87. Mule

88. Golden Boy

89. Junior

90. Schoolboy

91. Mad Russian

92. Scoops

93. Push-'em-Up	110. Hoolie
94. Happy Jack	111. Buggy Whip
95. Slats	112. Big Bear
96. Georgia Peach	113. Zeke
97. Scrap Iron	114. Hands
98. Big Cat	115. Fritz
99. Bucketfoot	116. Brooklyn Schoolboy
100. Colonel	117. Motormouth
101. Hawk	118. Three-Finger
102. Kitty	119. Kinny
103. Gabby	120. Cat
104. Pudge	121. Wee Willie
105. Rajah	122. Crab
106. Pinky	123. Boozie
107. Wahoo Sam	124. Tiger
108. King Carl	125. Rico
109. Dummy	126. Pop

3.
BALLPARKS

Name the home ballpark in which each of the following teams play.

1. Chicago Cubs _____

2. Minnesota Twins _____

3. Atlanta Braves _____

4. Montreal Expo's _____

5. Cincinnati Reds _____

6. San Francisco Giants _____

7. New York Mets _____

8. Boston Red Sox _____

9. Philadelphia Phillies _____

10. Baltimore Orioles _____

11. Pittsburgh Pirates _____

12. St. Louis Cardinals _____

13. California Angels _____

14. Cleveland Indians _____

15. Texas Rangers _____

4.

BASEBALL QUIZ

1. Who holds the ML record for most putouts and most chances handled by a first baseman in 1 extra-inning game?

2. Who was the only NL player to win the triple crown twice?

3. What is the record for most double plays started or assisted in, in a 9-inning game?

4. What is the record for most season pinch hits? Name player(s).

5. If a pinch hitter bats twice in 1 inning and gets 2 straight hits is he credited with 2 pinch hits?

6. Which baseball team was the first transported by airplane?

7. How many players are members of the 3,000-hit club?

8. Who was the oldest player to win a batting crown?

9. Who was the first manager of the N.Y. Mets?

10. Which team had the most players on their roster in 1 season?

11. What was the longest game ever played in the ML?

12. What year was the rule enacted prohibiting the use of a soiled baseball?

13. Who managed the Philadelphia Athletics from 1901 to 1950?

14. Name the players whose last names spelled backwards are the same if spelled properly?

15. Who in baseball is known as a "rubber arm?"

16. Name the catcher who holds the AL record of 5 passed balls in 1 game.

17. Babe Ruth hit a record 9 home runs in 1 week. Name the player who has since broken this record?

18. How many times has Brooks Robinson won the Golden Glove award?

19. During the 1946 season only 1 regular player was not struck out by Bob Feller. Who was this player?

20. Name the player who holds the record for most doubles in a double header.

21. What is the limit to the size of a catcher's glove?

22. Name the pitcher who walked 16 batters in his first ML appearance.

23. Who hit 3 home runs in 1 playoff game?

24. Name the first Chicago White Sox player to lead the AL in home runs.

25. In 1937 Frank Demaree was the last Cub player to get 6 straight hits in a game. Name the player who has since tied this record.

26. Who was the first player to hit 500 or more home runs and accumulate 3,000 or more hits?

27. Name the pitcher who won 28 games as a rookie.

28. Who holds the ML record for most total bases in a lifetime?

29. Who holds the ML record for most total bases in 1 game?

30. How was the ML record for most total bases in 1 game achieved?

31. How many career home runs did Ty Cobb hit?

32. How many career stolen bases did Babe Ruth have?

33. How many times did Willie Mays lead the NL in stolen bases?

34. Which team holds the record for most consecutive innings shutting out its opponents?

35. Who holds the record for most consecutive shut-out games in 1 season?

36. In 1965 Jack Fisher, Mets, lost 24 games in 1 season. Who was the other Mets pitcher who also lost 24 games in 1 season?

37. Which AL pitcher holds the record for the highest pitching percentage in 1 season?

38. What is the record for most assists by a catcher in a 9-inning game, since 1900?

39. How many times has a player hit 3 triples in a game?

40. Name the 3 players who hit over .400 in 2 consecutive years? Also name the teams for whom each played.

41. Who holds the record for most assists by a third baseman in 1 game?

42. Name the only ML player whose death was caused by being hit in the head by a pitched ball?

43. What is the record for a first baseman for most putouts in a 9-inning game?

44. Who was the founder of the Chicago White Sox?

45. Who holds the AL record for most shutouts pitched in 1 season?

46. What is the ML record for most assists by a shortstop in a 9-inning game?

47. Who holds the ML record for most triples in a lifetime?

48. Who holds the ML record for most assists by a shortstop in a lifetime?

49. Who holds the ML record for most RBI's in 1 season?

50. Who holds the ML record for most RBI's in a lifetime?

51. The St. Louis Cardinals were known as the "Gas House Gang." Who originated this team's name?

52. Who holds the NL record for most consecutive games hitting safely in 1 season?

53. Which NL pitcher had the highest winning percentage in 1973?

54. Since 1900 what is the ML record for most losses by a pitcher in 1 season?

55. How many triple plays did the Astro's make in 1971?

56. How many total bases did Joe Torre have when he led the NL in that category in 1971?

57. How are earned run averages (ERA) calculated?

58. Name the first player ever to be hit by a pitch twice in 1 inning?

59. What is the AL record for most errors by a pitcher in 1 game?

60. How much does an official baseball weigh?

61. Name the player who had the most official "at bats" without hitting a home run?

62. Which Boston Red Sox player won the triple crown in 1967?

63. Who was the "on deck" batter when Bobby Thompson (Giants) homered against the Dodgers in the playoff game in 1951?

64. How many times did Carl Yastrzemski lead the AL outfielders in assists?

65. What is the ML record for most times reaching first base in 1 inning?

66. Identify the first baseman Lou Gehrig replaced.

67. Who replaced Lou Gehrig at first base?

68. What is the record for most assists by an outfielder in a 9-inning game?

69. What is the record for a batter for most consecutive times facing the pitcher without an official time at bat?

70. Who was the only player ever to hit for more than 400 total bases per season in 5 seasons?

71. Name the players who hold the ML record for most hits in each of the following categories in one season since 1900: a. singles   b. doubles   c. triples

72. Who holds the ML record for most "at bats" in 1 season?

73. Who holds the ML record for the lowest slugging average in 1 season?

74. Who holds the ML record for most seasons playing in 150 or more games?

75. Who holds the ML record for most *consecutive* seasons playing 150 or more games?

76. Who holds the record for most games played in a lifetime?

77. What is the record for most runs scored in a lifetime?

78. What is the record for most "at bats" in an extra inning game?

79. Who holds the record for most hits in 1 season?

80. In what year did the Washington Senators become the Minnesota Twins?

81. Who holds the ML record for most consecutive games scoring?

82. What is the record for most putouts by a leftfielder in a 9-inning game? Who was the last player to accomplish this feat?

83. Who holds the ML record for most double plays by a catcher in 1 season?

84. What is the ML record for most runs scored by a player in 1 game?

85. Who was baseball's first triple crown winner?

86. What is the ML record for most double plays started by a catcher in 1 game?

87. Who holds the record for most seasons scoring 100 or more runs?

88. Who holds the record for most extra base hits in a lifetime?

89. Who holds the record for most 2-base hits in a lifetime?

90. What are the AL and NL records for most pinch hit home runs. Name the players who hold these league records.
    a. AL
    b. NL

91. Who holds the ML record for most consecutive seasons leading or tying in home runs?

92. Name the AL and NL player who holds the record in his respective league for most home runs hit at home in 1 season.
    a. AL
    b. NL

93. Name the AL and NL player who holds the record in his respective league for most home runs hit on the road?
    a. AL
    b. NL

94. Name the player who holds the ML record for most games hitting a home run right and left handed.

95. Who led the ML in sacrifice hits 4 consecutive years?

96. Name the AL and NL player who holds the record in his respective league for most sacrifice flies in 1 game.
   a. AL
   b. NL

97. Babe Ruth led the ML's 4 consecutive years, 1930–1933, in bases on balls. Who tied this record?

98. Name the players who hold the record for most intentional bases on balls in each of the following categories:
   a. lifetime
   b. most seasons (consecutive)
   c. season

99. Name the AL and NL player who led his respective league for most seasons hitting into double plays.
   a. AL
   b. NL

100. Who holds the record for most RBI's in 1 season for a rookie?

101. Name the AL and NL player who led his respective league for most strikeouts by a rookie in his rookie season?
   a. AL
   b. NL

102. Name the manager of the 1950 pennant-winning Phillies.

103. Name the Cy Young and MVP winners in the NL in 1973.
   a. Cy Young
   b. MVP

104. Name the Cy Young and MVP winners in the AL in 1973.
    a. Cy Young
    b. MVP

105. Who holds the AL record for most home runs by a shortstop in 1 season?

106. What is the AL record for most RBI's by a pitcher in 1 game?

107. Name the pitcher who was the victim of Babe Ruth's famed "called shot" home run?

108. Name the pitcher who gave up Ted Williams's first ML hit.

109. In the 42 years the Baseball Writers Association has given the MVP award, how many AL players were named unanimously?

110. Who are these unanimously named AL-MVP award winners?

111. How many AL pitchers have won the MVP award?

112. Who are these award-winning AL pitchers?

113. Name the 2 players who have played 9 positions in 1 game?

114. Who holds the highest lifetime slugging average?

115. During what period of time were bases on balls considered hits?

116. Who led the NL in home runs and RBI's in 1973?

117. Name the pitcher who holds the record for appearing in most games in 1 season?

118. How many career stolen bases does Willie Davis have as of 1973?

119. In 1962 Maury Wills stole a record 104 bases. How many times did he steal 3 or more bases in 1 game? How many times was he caught stealing?

120. In 1915 Ty Cobb stole 96 bases in 1 season. How many times did he steal 3 or more bases in 1 game? How many times was he caught stealing?

121. How many home runs did Roger Maris and Mickey Mantle hit combined in 1961?

122. In 1947 2 NL players each hit 51 home runs. One played for the Pirates, the other for the Giants. Who were they?

123. In 1927 Babe Ruth started his 60 home-run season (154 games) by hitting home run number 1 off Howard Ehmke of the Philadelphia A's. Name the pitcher who gave up home run number 60?

124. In 1961 Roger Maris started his 61 home-run season (163 games) by hitting home run number 1 off Paul Foytack of the Detroit Tigers. Name the pitcher who gave up home run number 61.

125. During Babe Ruth's 60 home-run season, how many times did he hit 2 or more home runs in 1 game?

126. During Roger Maris's 61 home-run season, how many times did he hit 2 or more home runs in 1 game?

127. At the end of the 1973 season, how many career home runs did Jim Wynn have?

128. How many double plays were made by Joe Tinker and Johnny Evers in the 4 years they played together?

129. What is the ML record for most times hitting into a double play in 1 game? Identify players with this dubious honor.

130. Name the AL player who ranks third on the list for most walks in 1 season. Only Babe Ruth and Ted Williams are ahead of him.

131. How many home runs did Rudy York hit in the month of August 1937?

132. Who has since tied Eddie Stanky's NL record of most bases on balls in 1 season?

133. Who holds the NL record for most consecutive games played?

134. Who hit the ball at the Polo Grounds that Willie Mays caught with his back to the plate that saved the game in the 1954 WS?

135. Who was the pitcher against whom Babe Ruth hit his first ML home run?

136. Name the 2 brothers who finished first and second in a batting championship?

137. Name the player whose .388 average in 1936 is the highest average attained by an AL shortstop.

138. Who holds the NL record for a rookie, hitting safely in 23 consecutive games?

139. Who was the first player ever to achieve the feat of an unassisted triple play?

140. In how many games did Ernie Banks participate as a Cub player?

141. What was Rip Sewell's famous change-of-pace pitch called?

142. Who pitched the then L.A. Angels first no-hitter in 1962?

143. Who holds the NL record for most games played by a catcher in his rookie season?

144. Who was the youngest player ever to win a batting title?

145. Who are the 2 players credited with starting the hit-and-run play?

146. Prior to Joe DiMaggio's 56-game hitting streak, what was the ML record?

147. What is the most runs scored by a team of which all runs were driven in by 1 player?

148. For what player was the cheer "Slide, Kelly, Slide" originated?

149. Which ballpark publicized the leftfield home-run area as "Greenberg Gardens"?

150. How many years must a player be inactive before he can be considered for the Hall of Fame?

151. Name the player who hit a grand slam home run in his first ML game.

152. Who was the youngest AL manager?

153. Who first introduced shin guards for catchers?

154. In 1931 the NL batting title was won by 7/10ths of a point, between 3 players. Who were the players and what were their averages?

155. What year were players first selected for the Hall of Fame?

156. Who were the first players enshrined in the Baseball Hall of Fame?

157. Since 1900 who holds the AL's highest batting average for 1 season?

158. Who hit 3 grand slam home runs in 1 month?

159. Who was the only player to hit 3 consecutive home runs in Griffith Stadium (Washington Senators)?

160. Whose hit (a double) knocked Don Newcombe out of the game in the 1951 playoffs (Giant vs. Dodgers) and brought relief pitcher Ralph Branca in to pitch to Bobby Thompson?

161. What is the ML record for most foul balls caught by a catcher in 1 game?

162. Who holds the ML record for most games caught by a catcher in a lifetime?

163. Who was the player best known as Babe Ruth's caddy?

164. Who was the player who pinch-hit for Babe Ruth on April 24, 1915?

165. Name the players in the AL and NL who hold the record for most times stealing home in 1 season?

166. Since 1900 what is the record for striking out the most batters in 1 game?

167. What is the AL record for most times reaching first base safely in a 9-inning game?

168. Name the pitcher who holds the record for being struck out the most times during a season?

169. Who, in 1970, broke up pitching bids for no-hit fame by Phil Niekro, Sonny Siebert, and Jim Rooker, with a hit in the ninth inning of each game?

170. Were there any lefthanded catchers in the major leagues?

171. What is the ML record for a pitcher for most RBI's in 1 game?

172. Who holds the ML record for most RBI's in a double header?

173. Who were the first umpires to be elected to the Hall of Fame?

174. For what ML team did the Japanese star, Masanori Murakami, pitch?

175. Who was the manager of the 1901 Washington Senators?

176. Name the AL batter who was hit by most pitches in 1970.

177. Who was the first NL president?

178. Who was the manager of the 1969 Seattle Pilots?

179. Who led the ML in runs scored in 1972?

180. Who holds the ML record for most chances by a second base-man in 1 game?

181. Who was the "Fireman of the Year" in the AL in 1966?

182. What is the record for most errors made in a double header by both teams?

183. In what ballpark did the Cardinals play prior to playing in Sportsman Park?

184. Who was the originator of the catcher's mask?

185. Who holds the AL record for most times being hit by pitches in a lifetime?

186. The diameter of a baseball bat cannot exceed how many inches?

187. How many games did the Yankees play from 1931 to 1935 without being shut out?

188. Which team hit the least number of home runs in 1 season?

189. What is the most bases on balls given up by both teams in 1 game?

190. In what year was the NL officially formed?

191. What is the record for most men left on base in a 9-inning game?

192. Who was the first 20-game winner for the Houston Astro's?

193. Which NL catcher led the league in passed balls in 1970?

194. Which former Red Sox player holds the team record for most consecutive games hitting safely?

195. Who was the first black player in the AL?

196. Who was the ML's first pinch hitter?

197. Which AL and NL teams hold the record in their respective league for most stolen bases in 1 season?

198. What is the record for the most putouts by an AL outfielder in 1 season?

199. Redland Field was better known as _____ ?

200. Who is the winningest active pitcher in the ML's?

201. What is the leftfield wall in Boston's Fenway Park called?

202. How many Cub players hit 20 or more home runs in 1958?

203. What is the record for most chances accepted by an AL outfielder in 1 season?

204. Name the pitching staff of the Orioles' famous "Kiddie Korps" (1960s).

205. Who was the back-up catcher behind Roy Campanella on the 1951–1957 Brooklyn Dodgers?

206. How many games did Virgil Trucks and Hal Newhouser win for the Detroit Tigers combined in 1944?

207. How old was Dazzy Vance when he won his first ML game?

208. Who holds the AL record for most games playing first base in a lifetime?

209. Who was the midget who pinch-hit in a game on July 19, 1951, against the Tigers? What was his uniform number?

210. Since 1900, who holds the NL record for most errors by a shortstop in a lifetime?

211. Since 1900, who was the first ML infielder to wear glasses?

212. Who was the last NL player to hit over .400?

213. For which ML team did Jim Thorpe first play?

214. Who led the NL in stolen bases in 1970?

215. Who before Carlton Fisk held the Boston Red Sox record for most home runs by a catcher?

216. Who held the ML record for most career home runs before Babe Ruth broke this record in 1922?

217. Which NL third baseman holds the record in a 154-game schedule for most double plays in 1 season?

218. Who holds the ML record for pitching 39 consecutive complete games in normal rotation in 1 season?

219. Who was the manager of the year in the AL in 1972?

220. How many career stolen bases did Luke Easter have?

221. In what year was the first game played in Ebbets Field?

222. Who was the winning pitcher in the first game played in Ebbets Field?

223. What is the NL record for a catcher for most consecutive games played without an error?

224. Who was the third baseman on the Indians whose 2 big plays on July 17, 1941, helped to end Joe DiMaggio's 56-game hitting streak?

225. Who got the first base hit in Comiskey Park, on July 1, 1910?

226. Who was the first NL player to invoke the baseball rule that a 10-year player with 5 years' tenure with the same team cannot be traded without his permission?

227. Who are the only NL players to win the MVP award 3 times?

228. Who was the only NL player to win the MVP award unanimously?

229. Who was the only player to win the MVP award 2 consecutive years?

230. What is the ML record for most unassisted double plays by a first baseman in 1 game?

231. In what year did baseball have its first player draft?

232. Who was the first player to win a batting title without hitting a home run all season?

233. Who was the first player to bat in the first night game?

234. Before becoming the Yankees the team was called the _____ ?

235. Who holds the NL record for most pinch hit home runs in 1 season?

236. Name the 2 former Yankee players elected to the Hall of Fame in 1974.

237. Who was the 46th player to play third base for the Mets?

238. Who was the 1-armed outfielder who played for the 1945 St. Louis Browns?

239. Among active AL players, who has the most career home runs?

240. En route to his 61 home runs in 1961, how many pitchers were nicked for 3 or more home runs by Roger Maris?

241. What is the ML record for most innings played in a night game? Name the teams who participated.

242. Who was the first NL player to earn $100,000 a year?

243. Who holds the NL record for most innings caught in 1 extra inning game?

244. Which AL player also an MVP award winner, led the league in strikeouts in 1968–1971?

245. In 1952, 2 NL sluggers were tied for the home-run title with 37 each. One played for the Cubs, the other for the Pirates. Who were they?

246. In 1963, 2 NL sluggers were tied for the home-run title with 44 each. One played for the Giants, the other for the Braves. Who were they?

247. In 1967, 2 AL sluggers were tied for the home-run title with 44 each. One played for the Red Sox, the other for the Twins. Who were they?

248. Who won the stolen base title in 1950 with the lowest winning total ever recorded?

249. How many times did Jackie Robinson lead the NL in stolen bases?

250. Name the player who led the 1918 ML season in bases on balls with the lowest winning total on record.

251. What was odd about Yankee outfielder Myril Hoag (played for Yankees, 1934–1938)?

252. In 1972, 2 NL players led the league with the most 2-base hits —39. One played for the Astro's, the other for the Phillies. Who were they?

253. In 1970, 3 AL players were tied for the league lead in 2-base hits with 36 each. One played for the K.C. Athletics, the other 2 for the Twins. Who were they?

254. In 1970, 2 NL players were tied for the league lead for most hits in a season with 205. One played for the Cubs, the other for the Reds. Who were they?

255. Who holds the ML record for most putouts by a second base-man in a double header?

256. Whom did Whitey Herzog relieve as manager of the Texas Rangers?

257. What is the ML record for most assists by an outfielder in 1 inning?

258. What was most unusual and may never happen again about the double play Jess Hill of the Yankees hit into on July 26, 1935?

259. Who was the manager of the 1963 Washington Senators?

260. Since 1900, who was the first player to win the home-run title and also had the fewest strikeouts that season?

261. Who was the rookie pitcher who pitched a no-hitter for the Chicago Cubs in 1972?

262. How can a game be won without a winning or losing pitcher?

263. Who holds the ML record for hitting the most home runs in 1 week?

264. What was Hank Aaron's 1973 slugging percentage?

265. How many plate appearances must a batter have to qualify for a batting title?

266. Which ML team was the first to have 3 players with 40 or more home runs each in 1 season?

267. Which AL and NL players share the ML record for striking out 100 or more times in 9 consecutive seasons?

268. Which NL player led the league in 1973 for most times being hit by a pitch?

269. Which Twins player led the league in home runs 3 straight years, 1962–1964? How many did he hit each year?

270. What is the AL record for most stolen bases in 1 season by a rookie?

271. Who was the player John McGraw called "My Greatest Outfielder"?

272. Who holds the AL record for most putouts by a third baseman in a lifetime?

273. Who was the player who committed the "$30,000 Muff"? This cost the Giants the World Series in 1912.

274. Whom did Fred Hutchinson replace as manager of the Tigers in 1952?

275. Who was the first ML player to use a glove?

276. Which team won the AL pennant in 1944?

277. Who was the first president of the AL?

278. Who led the NL in hitting into the most double plays during the 1970 season?

279. In 1906, which team was called the "Hitless Wonders"?

280. What former Tiger third baseman had his jaw fractured by a line drive off Joe DiMaggio's bat in 1948?

281. Which AL and NL teams won the most games in 1 season?

282. Mike Kilkenny started the 1972 season with the Tigers. To which other teams was he traded during the season?

283. Who holds the ML record for most errors by a catcher in a lifetime?

284. Who was the first baseball player to hold out for more money?

285. Who holds the record for the fastest time recorded in circling the bases?

286. Name the pitcher who gave up the tape measure home run to Mickey Mantle (565 ft.) at Griffith Stadium in 1956?

287. Who was the first player to wear sliding pads?

288. Who, while with the Red Sox in 1952–1953, was known as Ted Williams's caddy?

289. Whose home run on the last day of the 1950 season in the tenth inning wrapped up the pennant for the Phillies? The home run was hit off Don Newcombe, Dodgers.

290. Who was the backup catcher for the Yankees in 1948–1956 behind Yogi Berra?

291. Who was the manager of the Brooklyn Dodgers 1947–1950?

292. Since 1900, who holds the AL record for most hits in 1 inning?

293. Who was the third baseman in the Cubs infield that included the famous trio of Tinker, Evers, and Chance?

294. Who before Joe DiMaggio held the AL record for most consecutive games hitting safely since 1900?

295. Who was the stolen base leader in the AL in 1973?

296. In 1973, 2 players were tied for the lead for most 3-base hits during the season. One played for the Orioles, the other for the Twins. Who were they?

297. Who played centerfield for the Yankees while Joe DiMaggio was in the army 1943–1945?

298. Who wore Babe Ruth's number (3) before the number was retired?

299. Who hit the line drive in 1957 that struck Herb Score in the eye?

300. Who was the youngest player to play for an AL team?

301. Who is known as the "Clown Prince of Baseball"?

302. Who was the first player in the ML's to be both a pitcher and a catcher?

303. Who took over the catching duties for the Dodgers succeeding Roy Campanella?

304. What year did the Braves move from Boston to Milwaukee?

305. Who was the first NL rookie to hit 3 home runs in 1 game?

306. What is the NL record, and who holds it, for most chances accepted by a pitcher in 1 extra inning game?

307. What is the ML record, for a catcher, for catching most no-hit games?

308. The distance from the pitcher's mound to home plate is 60 ft. 6 in. What was the distance previously?

309. Who was the only player to get 5 hits in his first ML game? Name the team for which he played.

310. Who is the only player ever to lead both the AL and NL in home runs? Name the teams for which he played.

311. Who holds the AL record for most RBI's in 1 season?

312. Who holds the NL record for most consecutive years with 150 or more RBI's?

313. Who was the first player ever to hit 3 home runs in 1 game?

314. Who was the first AL player to hit 3 home runs in 1 game?

315. Who holds the AL record, for a catcher, for most runners thrown out trying to steal in a 9-inning game?

316. Who was the first player to hit 3 home runs in a game in both the AL and NL?

317. Since 1900, what is the AL record, for 1 player, for most consecutive games scoring a run?

318. Since 1900, what is the NL record, for 1 player, for most consecutive games scoring a run?

319. Who is the only player ever to lead his league in home runs, triples, and doubles in the same season? For whom did he play?

320. Who has been credited with inventing the chest protector?

321. Who holds the ML record for most hits in a season by a right-handed batter?

322. Who was the first player ever to hit 4 home runs in 1 game? For whom did he play?

323. What is and who holds the AL record for most consecutive games played by an outfielder?

324. Who hit the first official home run in ML history?

325. Which ML team made 2 triple plays on successive days (June 6, 1908, and June 7, 1908)?

326. Who hit the first home run in Yankee Stadium?

327. What was the price of the first paid admission to a ball game?

328. What is the average number of pitches thrown by a pitcher in a 9-inning game?

329. When was the first game played at Yankee Stadium?

330. Who was the first Yankee player to bat at Yankee Stadium?

331. Who was the first Yankee pitcher ever to pitch a game in Yankee Stadium?

332. Ten Cardinal players have won the NL-MVP award. How many of these award winners can you name?

333. Nine Yankee players have won the AL-MVP award. How many of these award winners can you name?

334. What did Joe DiMaggio do in his last "at bat" that ended his 56-game hitting streak?

335. In 1961, how many home runs did Roger Maris hit through game number 154?

336. On Oct 2, 1961, Roger Maris hit home run number 61 against the Red Sox. This hit not only made history but was the game-winning run. What was the final score of this game?

337. During Babe Ruth's 60-home-run season and Roger Maris's 61-home-run season, how many plate appearances and how many official "at bats" did each have?

338. In 1938 Hank Greenberg had the best chance of hitting 60 or more home runs in a 154-game season. When he hit home run number 58, how many games did he have left to play that season?

339. Who was the first AL catcher named Rookie of the Year?

340. Who was the first NL catcher named Rookie of the Year?

341. Name the AL teams who came in first in their divisions in 1973, East and West.

342. Name the NL teams who came in first in their divisions in 1973, East and West.

343. When was the first game played that went into the official league records?

344. Which team won a season opener because of a forfeit?

345. Which NL team opens its season every year at its home ball-park while other teams have opening day at home on alternate years?

346. Who holds the Mets team record for most total bases in 1 game?

347. Who was the first ML player to hit 50 or more home runs and steal 20 or more bases in the same season?

5.

PITCHING QUIZ

1. How many no-hit games did Sandy Koufax pitch?

2. How many no-hit and 1-hit games did Bob Feller pitch?

3. Name the ML pitchers who have pitched 2 no-hit games in 1 season.

4. Name the pitchers since 1900 who have pitched a perfect regular-season game. Also name team opponents.

5. Name the pitcher who retired 36 batters in a row only to lose a no-hitter and the game in the 13th inning.

6. What is the ML record for most unassisted double plays by a pitcher?

7. Name the NL pitcher who holds the record for highest won-and-lost percentage in 1 season (15 decisions or more).

8. Elroy Face's best pitch was his _____ .

9. How many games did Cy Young win in his lifetime?

10. Who holds the AL and NL record for pitchers, leading the league in games won for most consecutive seasons?

11. Who holds the record for the most consecutive seasons leading ML in games won?

12. Name the pitcher who holds the record for most games finished in a lifetime.

13. Name the pitcher who holds the NL record for most games finished in the league.

14. Name the AL and NL pitchers who have given up the most earned runs in a lifetime.

15. Name the AL and NL pitchers who have given up the most earned runs in a season.

16. What is the AL and NL record for most runs scored in an inning off 1 pitcher.

17. Name the AL and NL pitchers who hold their league records for the most balks in 1 game.

18. Name the AL and NL pitchers who hold their league records for the most balks in a season.

19. Name the pitcher who holds the ML record for the most wild pitches in 1 inning.

20. Since 1900, who holds the AL and NL records for most wild pitches in 1 game?

21. What are the AL and NL records for most wild pitches in a lifetime?

22. Who holds the AL and NL records for most bases on balls given up in 1 season since 1900?

23. Name the pitcher who holds the record for most bases on balls given up in an extra-inning game.

24. Who was the only pitcher ever to win 27 games with a team finishing a season in last place?

25. Steve Carlton struck out 19 Met batters on September 15, 1969, but lost the game as 1 batter hit 2 2-run homers during the game. Who was this batter?

26. Who was the pitcher whose only complete game in the ML was a no-hitter?

27. Which NL pitcher led the league in shutouts in 1972?

28. Who was baseball's first pitcher to win 200 games?

29. Which ML pitcher has been known to soak his pitching hand in pickle juice to eliminate blisters on his fingers?

30. Who pitched the entire game for the Brooklyn Dodgers that went 26 innings (against Braves)?

31. Who set the record for most innings pitched by a relief pitcher, finishing a single game?

32. Who holds the ML record for pitching the longest shutout?

33. What is the ML record for most innings pitched in a season, since 1900?

34. Which AL pitcher in 1973 led the league in shutouts?

35. How many no-hitters were pitched in the AL in 1973?

36. Name the pitchers who pitched no-hitters in the AL in 1973.

37. In 1973 how many AL pitchers won 20 or more games?

38. How many AL 20-game winners in 1973 can you name?

39. Who in the AL in 1973 set a new ML record for a relief pitcher for most games saved in 1 season?

40. Who pitched the most complete games in the AL during the 1973 season?

41. Which AL pitcher led the league in games started in 1973?

42. Name the 2 AL rookies who pitched no-hitters during the 1973 season?

43. Which AL pitcher in 1973 led the league in most innings pitched, most runs allowed, and most hits allowed?

44. Which NL pitcher won the most games in 1973?

45. Which AL pitcher won the most games in 1973?

46. Since 1900, name the AL pitcher who completed the most games in 1 season.

47. Since 1900, name the NL pitcher who completed the most games in 1 season.

48. Since 1900, what is the ML record for most batters faced by a pitcher in 1 inning? Name the last pitcher to equal this mark.

49. Name the 1959 Tiger pitcher who allowed the most home runs with the bases loaded in 1 season.

50. Name the NL pitcher who hurled for the Pirates and has allowed the most home runs with the bases loaded in a lifetime.

51. Name the AL pitcher who in a lifetime has allowed the most home runs with the bases loaded?

52. Since 1900, name the AL hurler who has allowed the most hits in the league in a lifetime?

53. Since 1900, name the NL pitcher who has allowed the most hits in the league in a lifetime?

54. Name the AL pitcher who has allowed the most home runs in a lifetime.

55. Name the NL pitcher who has allowed the most home runs in a lifetime.

56. Name the AL pitcher who has allowed the most home runs in 1 season. He pitched for the Senators in 1957.

57. Name the NL pitcher who has allowed the most home runs in 1 season. He pitched for the Phillies in 1956.

58. Name the AL pitcher with the Senators, 1907–1927, who holds the league record for hitting most batters with pitches in a lifetime.

59. Name the NL pitcher with the Dodgers, 1956–1969, who holds the league record for hitting most batters with pitches in a lifetime.

60. Name the AL relief pitcher who holds the record for most games won in 1 season.

61. Name the NL relief pitcher who holds the record for most games won in 1 season.

6.

ALL-STAR GAME QUIZ

1. How many grand-slam home runs have been hit in All-Star games?

2. How many years were 2 All-Star games played?

3. Where was the first All-Star game played?

4. Which team won the first All-Star game?

5. Name the winning and losing pitchers of the first All-Star game.

6. Name the managers of the first All-Star contest.

7. Name the AL and NL players who hit home runs in the 1933 All-Star game.

8. Name the player who has appeared in the most All-Star games.

9. Who holds the record for most total bases in 1 All-Star game?

10. Three players since 1933 have gotten 4 hits in an All-Star game. The first was Joe Medwick, 1937; second was Ted Williams, 1946. Who was the third player to achieve this feat?

11. Name the 4 players who hit 2 home runs in an All-Star game. Name the teams for whom they played.

12. What is the record for most RBI's in one All-Star game?

13. What batter holds the record for most strikeouts in 1 All-Star game?

14. Who holds the record for most strikeouts (batter) in All-Star competition in a lifetime?

15. Name the player who has scored the most runs in All-Star competition.

16. Who are the AL and NL players who have received 3 bases on balls in 1 All-Star game?

17. Name the AL and NL pitchers who have pitched most innings in 1 All-Star game.

18. What is the record for most earned runs given up in 1 All-Star game?

19. Name the pitcher who holds the record for most consecutive strikeouts, in 1 All-Star game.

20. Who holds the record for the highest lifetime batting average in All-Star competition?

21. Who are the AL and NL pitchers who have appeared in the most consecutive All-Star games?

22. Who holds the record for the most strikeouts (pitcher), lifetime, in All-Star competition?

23. Name the AL pitcher who holds the record for most strikeouts, lifetime, in All-Star contests.

24. Name the AL and NL pitchers who hold the record for most innings pitched, lifetime, in All-Star competition.

25. Who holds the AL and NL record for most runs given up in All-Star games in a lifetime?

26. Name the AL and NL pitchers who have allowed the most hits, lifetime, in All-Star competition?

27. Name the AL and NL pitchers who hold the record for most wild pitches (2) in All-Star competition.

28. Who holds the record for most walks given up in 1 inning of an All-Star game?

29. Since 1933, when the first All-Star game was played, through 1973, in what year was a game not played?

30. Who holds the record for most stolen bases in All-Star competition, 1 game and lifetime?

31. Name the player who has been caught stealing most times in 1 All-Star game.

32. Name the AL and NL players who have appeared on most winning All-Star teams.

33. Name the AL and NL players who have appeared on most losing All-Star teams.

34. Name the AL and NL players who have the most hits, lifetime, in All-Star competition.

35. The most hits for an individual batter in 1 All-Star game is 4. How many AL and NL players can you name who have achieved this feat?

36. Who holds the NL record for most strikeouts (batter), lifetime, in All-Star competition?

37. Name the player who has appeared in most consecutive All-Star games.

38. What is the record for most official at bats in 1 All-Star game?

39. Hank Aaron hit his first All-Star game home run in 1971. Who was the pitcher?

40. Who was the only rookie to play on the 1972 All-Star AL team?

41. Who drove in the winning run for the NL in the 1970 All-Star game?

42. Who was the only player ever to hit a home run off Rip Sewell's "Eephus" pitch in an All-Star game?

43. Who was the losing pitcher in the 1955 All-Star game when Stan Musial hit a home run to win the game in the twelfth inning?

44. Who was the winning pitcher of that same game?

45. Who was the winning pitcher of the rain-shortened All-Star game in 1952?

46. Who was the losing pitcher of that game?

7.

WORLD SERIES QUIZ

1. Since 1903, how many times has there not been a WS?

2. Who was the pitching hero of the first WS played in 1903? For which team did he pitch?

3. Lou Brock twice stole 3 bases in a WS—once against the Red Sox in 1967. Name the other team against whom he also stole 3 bases.

4. Name the player who has played in 75 WS games.

5. How many home runs did Mickey Mantle hit in WS competition?

6. In how many WS did Yogi Berra participate?

7. How many WS games ended in a tie?

8. Which team appeared in the most WS contests?

9. How many teams can you name that have appeared in WS competition but have never won the series?

10. What is the record for most runs scored by a team in WS competition?

11. Of the 29 WS in which the Yankees appeared, how many series did they win and lose?

12. What is the WS record for most bases stolen in each of the following categories:
    a. 4-game WS
    b. 5-game WS
    c. 6-game WS
    d. 7-game WS

13. What is the WS record for most runs scored in a game by both teams?

14. What is the WS record for most earned runs scored in 1 game?

15. What is the WS record for most runs scored in 1 game by 1 team?

16. Which team holds the WS record for most RBI's?

17. What is the WS record for most RBI's by both teams in 1 inning?

18. Name the players who hold the WS record for most RBI's in each of the following categories:
    a. 4-game WS
    b. 5-game WS
    c. 6-game WS
    d. 7-game WS

19. What is the WS record for most RBI's by both teams in 1 game?

20. What is the WS record for most RBI's by 1 team in 1 inning?

21. What is the total WS record for most hits by 1 team?

22. What is the WS record for most hits by both teams in 1 game?

23. What is the WS record for most total bases in 1 game?

24. What is the WS record for most total bases by both teams in 1 game?

25. What is the WS record for most total bases by both teams in 1 inning?

26. Which team holds the WS record for most home runs in a half inning?

27. Name the player who holds the record for most WS hits in a lifetime.

28. Name the 2 NL teams who share the WS record for most hits by 1 team in 1 game?

29. What is the WS record for most hits by a team in 1 inning?

30. What is the WS record for consecutive hits by a team in 1 inning?

31. Name the players who hold the WS record for most hits, in a WS, in each of the following categories:
    a. 4-game WS
    b. 5-game WS
    c. 6-game WS
    d. 7-game WS

32. Name the players who hold the record for the highest slugging average, in a WS, in each of the following categories:
    a. 4-game WS
    b. 5-game WS
    c. 6-game WS
    d. 7-game WS

33. Name the players who hold the WS record for most total bases, in a WS, in each of the following categories:
    a. 4-game WS
    b. 5-game WS
    c. 6-game WS
    d. 7-game WS

34. Name the players who hold the WS record for most home runs, in a WS, in each of the following categories:
    a. 4-game WS
    b. 5-game WS
    c. 6-game WS
    d. 7-game WS

35. Name the players who hold the WS record for most bases on balls, in a WS, in each of the following categories:
   a. 4-game WS
   b. 5-game WS
   c. 6-game WS
   d. 7-game WS

36. Name the players who hold the WS record for the highest batting average, in a WS, in each of the following categories:
   a. 4-game WS
   b. 5-game WS
   c. 6-game WS
   d. 7-game WS

37. Name the players who hold the WS record for having struck out most times, in a WS, in each of the following categories:
   a. 4-game WS
   b. 5-game WS
   c. 6-game WS
   d. 7-game WS

38. Of the 71 base hits Yogi Berra had in WS competition, how many hits were singles?

39. In 1969, name the Mets player who hit a game-tying home run that enabled them to defeat the Orioles in the final game?

40. Who was the first player to hit a grand-slam home run in WS history?

41. Which former Yankee player hit safely in 17 consecutive WS games?

42. Who broke up Bill Bevens's (Yankees) bid for a WS no-hitter in the ninth inning of the 1947 WS (Dodgers vs. Yankees)?

43. Who was the first black pitcher to win a WS game?

44. Who was the first left-handed pitcher to win 3 WS games in 1 series?

45. Who was the catcher in the 1941 WS charged with a passed ball error that resulted in the loss of the game?

46. What was Roberto Clemente's WS career batting average?

47. What is the record for most triples in 1 WS game for a player?

48. Identify player who holds the record for most errors in 1 inning.

49. Name the pitcher and the batter in that 1941 WS game that was lost because of a passed ball. What was the count on the batter?

50. Who is the only player to make an unassisted triple play in a WS game?

51. Who hit the home run in the ninth inning of the final game of the 1960 WS in which the Pirates defeated the Yankees?

52. How many runs did Gene Tenace drive in during the 1972 WS (A's vs. Reds)?

53. Who was the losing manager in the first WS in 1903?

54. As a pitcher, how many WS innings did Babe Ruth pitch without allowing a run?

55. Who is the only player to hit better than .300 in 4 consecutive WS?

56. Who holds the WS record for most innings pitched without allowing a run?

57. Who was the first NL player to hit a grand-slam home run in a WS game?

58. Can you name the 4 "big" pitchers from the staff of the 1945 champion Cubs?

59. Who were the 2 pitchers (brothers) who won all 4 WS games in 1934?

60. Who hit the game-winning home run in the first and third games of the 1923 WS?

61. Who pitched 3 shutouts in the 1905 WS?

62. After the 1919 WS, 8 players were banned from baseball for game-fixing. What was this scandal called?

63. Who hit the first WS home run in Yankee Stadium?

64. Who scored the run in the 1962 WS that ended Whitey Ford's WS record of 33-2/3 scoreless innings?

65. When Don Larsen pitched his perfect WS game, who was the last batter he faced, and what did this batter do?

8.

ROOKIE-OF-THE-YEAR QUIZ

AL: The year and team they played for are listed. Name the player.

1.	1949	St. Louis Browns	_____
2.	1950	Boston Red Sox	_____
3.	1951	New York Yankees	_____
4.	1952	Philadelphia Athletics	_____
5.	1953	Detroit Tigers	_____
6.	1954	New York Yankees	_____
7.	1955	Cleveland Indians	_____
8.	1956	Chicago White Sox	_____
9.	1957	New York Yankees	_____
10.	1958	Washington Senators	_____
11.	1959	Washington Senators	_____
12.	1960	Baltimore Orioles	_____
13.	1961	Boston Red Sox	_____
14.	1962	New York Yankees	_____
15.	1963	Chicago White Sox	_____
16.	1964	Minnesota Twins	_____
17.	1965	Baltimore Orioles	_____
18.	1966	Chicago White Sox	_____
19.	1967	Minnesota Twins	_____
20.	1968	New York Yankees	_____
21.	1969	Kansas City Royals	_____
22.	1970	New York Yankees	_____
23.	1971	Cleveland Indians	_____
24.	1972	Boston Red Sox	_____
25.	1973	Baltimore Orioles	_____

NL: The year and team they played for are listed. Name the player.

1. 1949   Brooklyn Dodgers   _____
2. 1950   Boston Braves   _____
3. 1951   New York Giants   _____
4. 1952   Brooklyn Dodgers   _____
5. 1953   Brooklyn Dodgers   _____
6. 1954   St. Louis Cardinals   _____
7. 1955   St. Louis Cardinals   _____
8. 1956   Cincinnati Reds   _____
9. 1957   Philadelphia Phillies   _____
10. 1958 San Francisco Giants   _____
11. 1959 San Francisco Giants   _____
12. 1960 Los Angeles Dodgers   _____
13. 1961 Chicago Cubs   _____
14. 1962 Chicago Cubs   _____
15. 1963 Cincinnati Reds   _____
16. 1964 Philadelphia Phillies   _____
17. 1965 Los Angeles Dodgers   _____
18. 1966 Cincinnati Reds   _____
19. 1967 New York Mets   _____
20. 1968 Cincinnati Reds   _____
21. 1969 Los Angeles Dodgers   _____
22. 1970 Montreal Expo's   _____
23. 1971 Atlanta Braves   _____
24. 1972 New York Mets   _____
25. 1973 San Francisco Giants   _____

9.

HOME RUN LEADERS BY POSITION— SEASON AND LIFETIME

How many players can you name who hold the AL and NL records for most home runs by position in 1 season and lifetime? The number of home runs hit are helpful hints.

AL—SEASON

POSITION	HR	PLAYER
Pitcher	9	_____
Catcher	30	_____
First Base	58	_____
Second Base	32	_____
Third Base	43	_____
Shortstop	40	_____
Outfield	61	_____

NL—SEASON

POSITION	HR	PLAYER
Pitcher	7	_____
Catcher	40	_____
First Base	51	_____
Second Base	43	_____
Third Base	47	_____
Shortstop	47	_____
Outfield	56	_____

AL—LIFETIME

POSITION	HR	PLAYER
Pitcher	37	
Catcher	313	
First Base	493	
Second Base	253	
Third Base	242	
Shortstop	247	
Outfield	699	

NL—LIFETIME

POSITION	HR	PLAYER
Pitcher	35	
Catcher	242	
First Base	355	
Second Base	299	
Third Base	483	
Shortstop	293	
Outfield	643	

10.
ALL-TIME TEAM HOME RUN LEADERS

The year, team, and number of home runs are indicated. Name the player.

	YEAR	TEAM	HR	PLAYER
1.	1929	Philadelphia Phillies (NL)	43	_____
2.	1930	Chicago Cubs (NL)	56	_____
3.	1938	Detroit Tigers (AL)	58	_____
4.	1938	Boston Red Sox (AL)	50	_____
5.	1940	St. Louis Cardinals (NL)	43	_____
6.	1949	Pittsburgh Pirates (NL)	54	_____
7.	1953	Cleveland Indians (AL)	43	_____
8.	1954	Cincinnati Reds (NL)	49	_____
9.	1961	New York Yankees (AL)	61	_____
10.	1962	New York Mets (NL)	34	_____
11.	1962	California Angels (AL)	37	_____
12.	1962	Los Angeles Dodgers (NL)	31	_____
13.	1964	Minnesota Twins (AL)	49	_____
14.	1965	San Francisco Giants (NL)	52	_____

	YEAR	TEAM	HR	PLAYER
15.	1966	Baltimore Orioles (AL)	49	_____
16.	1967	Houston Astros (NL)	37	_____
17.	1969	Washington Senators (AL)	48	_____
18.	1969	Oakland A's (AL)	47	_____
19.	1970	San Diego Padres (AL)	38	_____
20.	1970	Milwaukee Brewers (AL)	31	_____
21.	1970	Kansas City Royals (AL)	27	_____
22.	1970	Montreal Expo's (NL)	30	_____
23.	1971	Atlanta Braves (NL)	47	_____
24.	1972	Chicago White Sox (AL)	37	_____

11.

BASEBALL TERMINOLOGY (SLANG)

Fill in the blank with a word or phrase that describes each particular fact or situation.

1. Advancing a runner 1 base: _____
2. A short fly ball that drops between outfielder and infielder: _____
3. A batter who hits to all fields: _____
4. Lay it down: _____
5. Flutter ball: _____
6. A player who comes to bat during game but did not start: _____
7. Batter slaps ball to opposite field advancing runner from first to third: _____
8. A key hit that scores winning run: _____
9. What is the area called where pitchers warm up during game: _____
10. Sliding into a base: _____
11. Stealing "home" while batter positions himself to bunt: _____
12. A pitch that takes off: _____
13. A pitcher who throws from below the waistline: _____
14. Third base is also called: _____
15. Hitting a home run with three runners on base: _____

16. Hitting a home run with no one on base: _____

17. Coming through with the hit that ties or decides game:
_____

18. A ball that is hit between the legs, dropped, or overthrown:
_____

19. What is the fielder called who receives ball from outfielder prior to ball arriving at a base: _____

20. When a pitcher leaves a game during an inning, he is going where: _____

21. A pitched ball thrown wide of or over the catcher's head:
_____

22. A pitch that the catcher fails to handle: _____

23. A batter reaching first base on 4 balls: _____

24. The way strikeouts are recorded on scorecards: _____

25. A hit that scores a run is credited to the batter as:
_____

26. A fly ball that is caught but scores a run: _____

27. An infield hit that takes a high bounce: _____

28. A batted ball that removes lead runner from basepath and places batter on first: _____

29. A batter who hits both lefthanded and righthanded:
_____

30. A game going beyond 9 innings: _____

12.

BASEBALL SCORE SHEET QUIZ

Recording plays on a score sheet by means of baseball shorthand can make every game more enjoyable. How well do you know the system and symbols used?

A. What are the numbers used for players by field position?

1. Right fielder _____   6. Shortstop _____

2. First baseman _____   7. Pitcher _____

3. Catcher _____   8. Third baseman _____

4. Second baseman _____   9. Center fielder _____

5. Left fielder _____

B. What do the symbols listed below represent?

1. – _____   9. BB _____

2. E _____   10. SH _____

3. FC _____   11. = _____

4. HP _____   12. PB _____

5. ≡ _____   13. BK _____

6. S _____   14. ≡ _____

7. K _____   15. WP _____

8. FO _____   16. PH _____

C. Now that you know the players' numbers by field position and the symbols used for plays, here are some problems that you can try to work out.

Consider the lower left-hand corner of the score-sheet diamond home plate. Proceed counter clockwise towards first base, lower right-hand corner. Upper right-hand corner is second base, and third base is the upper left-hand corner. Follow the example above:

Batter reaches first base on an error by the third baseman, steals second, and goes to third on a wild pitch. He then scores on a passed ball.

To keep track of scoring, circle scoring plays at the home plate position. To keep track of outs, circle the out in the center of the diamond and indicate the field position number of the player(s) handling the chance.

1. Batter reaches first base on a single, goes to second on a balk, and reaches third on a passed ball. He then steals home and scores.

2. Batter strikes out.

3. Batter hits a double.

4. Batter hits a triple. He then scores on a wild pitch.

5. Batter reaches first base on a walk. He is called out at second on a force play.

6. Batter flies out to center fielder.

7. Batter hits ball to right field but reaches second base as fielder drops ball.

8. Batter grounds out, shortstop to first base.

9. Batter hits into a double play, second to short to first.

10. Batter grounds out, second to first.

11. Batter hits a double. He goes to third on a passed ball and scores on a throwing error by the catcher.

12. Batter singles to right field. He steals second base, and goes to third on error by the shortstop.

13.

CY YOUNG
AWARD WINNERS
PUZZLE

Find the Cy Young Award winners in the puzzle. The year they won the award and the team they played for are indicated. Their names appear in the puzzle and are spelled vertically, horizontally, forwards, backwards, and diagonally. When you find their names, circle them.

From 1956 through 1966 there was only 1 winner taken from both leagues. From 1967 to 1973 there were winners in each league.

1. 1956—Dodgers
2. 1957—Braves
3. 1958—Yankees
4. 1959—White Sox
5. 1960—Pirates

6. 1961—Yankees
7. 1962—Dodgers
8. 1963—Dodgers
9. 1964—Angels
10. 1965
    1966 —Dodgers (same player)

AL (1967–1973)

1. 1967—Red Sox
2. 1968—Tigers
3. 1969—Orioles
          Tigers —(tie)
4. 1970—Twins
5. 1971—A's
6. 1972—Indians
7. 1973—Orioles

NL (1967–1973)

1. 1967—Giants
2. 1968—Cardinals
3. 1969—Mets
4. 1970—Cardinals
5. 1971—Cubs
6. 1972—Phillies
7. 1973—Mets

```
T C B G A Y L O R D P E R R Y R O Q Z N L W A L H O C J K E
O S F I E L M Z O E L H O A P Z O L B E N I K B L Z W X A P
L A B H O K P L H N O X P R S U M N E I Z T O A N L E O G A
H N O L Z U D O N N E W C O M B E V A N P Q P L Z T A B Z L
Z D U O H I M T B Y L Z J I M P A L M E R O K R S B R E T Z
H Y B E L M E Q R M S T L O R T C H B T U O L Z T A L C L W
I K Z V E L K U E C T W N J I M L O N B O R G I E L Y B C A
B O B G I B S O N L E O T O Y B W Z V U E Z M H V E W L Y T
P U K L E D P M Z A T E A N V K R O U V L M T L E O Y W R E
G F A V K L A B N I E O N L N K V Y I E T V U Z C R N Z R L
H A L U I T A B E N O E W K A V E L E N U G V E A K N E E P
E X A M N A T I L V D E N A T L E B V R G T L R R E O O P E
T L O U M O A L V U E L O O R V K C B E I F E G L E M V M H
A E V F H G H O M O E R G U E R P Y L O F V G H T O R E I S
M A E P S W L D O L A E T P N G E H O L A V U E O P H I J N
P E R F O R M E L M K B E O H L A N L E K U T A N E O R O I
S A N T E R C A F P O K E R U L T E S A L N L O K U N E C K
H U O L A W E N E B E E R R L O R M E P W B O K E R T E E N
O M N E L C H C O V G H I K M E O C O V A K D E L V U T T E
M O L A N N E H I O P T C U B T A C P H L H O M E G V E O J
E L A N E O R A H W L E A B C N M P O K U S N S L B C G I N
N E W S T S A N D Y K O U F A X E Z L B T W D O E C E P N O
S U N L C B P C E O L E T N M I K E M C C O R M I C K E W S
A V O N L I T E G H I M E V Z H O L E T C K Y R S L E E P U
N A C K E G F O L O T S W H O L T R A K L V S T O M A P S G
T O V U L B K P R E S I T O N T W L N O N K D E A L S P A R
A L O V A O M T W H I T E Y F O R D E S K E A R V U N T A E
C U E S U B R W H I V L B C E V H L A O N K L U C A O W E F
L O R E V A E S M O T I V A N E M I K E C U E L L A R P O V
B L O U T E R O V L I K E R U W A K O L C L U E S V U E S A
```

14.

AMERICAN LEAGUE MVP
AWARD WINNERS PUZZLE

Find the AL MVP Award winners in the puzzle. The year(s) they won
the award and the team they played for are indicated. Their names
appear in the puzzle and are spelled vertically, horizontally, forwards, backwards, and diagonally. When you find their names, circle them.

1. 1931—Philadelphia A's
2. 1932,
   1933—Philadelphia A's,
   1938—Boston Red Sox
3. 1934—Detroit Tigers
4. 1935,
   1940—Detroit Tigers
5. 1936—New York Yankees
6. 1937—Detroit Tigers
7. 1939,
   1941,
   1947—New York Yankees
8. 1942—New York Yankees
9. 1943—New York Yankees
10. 1944,
    1945—Detroit Tigers
11. 1946,
    1949—Boston Red Sox
12. 1948—Cleveland Indians
13. 1950—New York Yankees
14. 1951,
    1954,
    1955—New York Yankees

15. 1952—Philadelphia A's
16. 1953—Cleveland Indians
17. 1956,
    1957,
    1962—New York Yankees
18. 1958—Boston Red Sox
19. 1959—Chicago White Sox
20. 1960,
    1961—New York Yankees
21. 1963—New York Yankees
22. 1964—Baltimore Orioles
23. 1965—Minnesota Twins
24. 1966—Baltimore Orioles
25. 1967—Boston Red Sox
26. 1968—Detroit Tigers
27. 1969—Minnesota Twins
28. 1970—Baltimore Orioles
29. 1971—Oakland A's
30. 1972—Chicago White Sox
31. 1973—Oakland A's

```
A L T O O E R O I H A N K G R E E N B E R G P O V W N K O L E L O F A
O L A D E N N I S M C L A I N T L O F U R E G G I E J A C K S O N A N
M V K L P O N D E R S T R P K W N B R E A L T V D S K E V T E U R S E
L O T J E V L E F T Y G R O V E M O N Y L W O N A G E A O R E G I K Z
J O E G O R D O N E P R E T S O L V T W G O R L B C A N Q E T E A N S
Z E K L O E P R T K O M I C K E Y M A N T L E S L M N Q O S R H L A V
A B T K O Z D R E T L I K V R E N L T W N O V P U R O R M U T R E L H
C A T Z F R L I R I Q Z O T K R E A N T V L O T E B R A L O C I D O R
A T E R O G E R M A R I S T V K R L V O Q R D B C D I K T H O G S K E
R U N C K L P R T A Z K O A T R I K O M V Z R E H L T O M W V R K E C
L O A N S R O K U C G L A T E S W Q R K V E O T L T R M O E V A L K E
Y E A R Z K Q T D O A G E B R I T E R O K R O I C D K N E N S T R E R
A B K L V W N O J A C K I E J E N S E N T O W E L O C C K L A N T R E
S O O N A S Y O L K T G L O H E R O S T R D R E N O C V K A L H O E L
T O N B E A G H I E O B L K O T U V N Z E K R L A B V T S H O P S D D
R U T N S P O H O Y T K Z E L L A K S T E V A D K U S E G Q T R A I N
Z A P S T H U Q S W N K R C H A R L I E G E H R I N G E R V U R T C A
E M S K T R A N O R O T O W Q H N L K O A C D B G H L O P S O E C K H
M I T A W N Z N Q C D T E F L O K U M R E S T O V Z W R O K A C L A C
S A N K Y R L H T A U V L T O F E R H L O C D Q T A B C R E N L B L D
K A L L A N H R O Z U L O V W R E K G Q A U R O R O Z I P E O R L L U
I K O N O R E T Z S M N V U O A K T O A R E A R O L F L T Z S P E E P
B U L L O K O I T M O P E A T N K R Q T Z A W E R O Q S T V N L O N S
T A L O V E R K R T W M N O E K A B K T S Q O N R V T S L I I P A B L
O B E V T L T A B Z Q T S W N R L K G H U T H U U D S N P O B O K S T
N O W O I T U M N T S X O F N O S L E N E V N E L K U B L F O T K L A
L K O H V V L E Q C X O S E K B L E A K S T O Q U T Z O R E R E A T S
O M P L O L O E H O A X O N T I M A Z K W Q T S A B S R B H S H A E L
V V G E C C N F F F W B T O P N O A K T N O S P Z K L R O U K U C S E
K T O A K K I Y R F N M L Z K S E R V N K I L F B D C K L N O C A L L
L Q O V O L M A I L T Q E A L O M A T R N K E N R Q K E P R O L Y S E
O C B T O M C E L T Q B C R T N E A V T O V K R C K P L O E R O P E S
P K S K I O K A O U R L K G H A P U Q C A E E F R Q C K N O B R O S E
E L L J O N L H A R M O N K I L L E B R E W W S A A T S Q R O O T A S
S E T W E S K L M O N E N A R H C O C Y E K C I M E Q C B A N T A S E
```

15.

NATIONAL LEAGUE MVP
AWARD WINNERS PUZZLE

Find the NL MVP Award winners in the puzzle. The year(s) they won
the award and the team they played for are indicated. Their names
appear in the puzzle and are spelled vertically, horizontally, forwards, backwards, and diagonally. When you find their names, circle them.

1. 1931—St. Louis Cardinals
2. 1932—Philadelphia Phillies
3. 1933,
   1936—New York Giants
4. 1934—St. Louis Cardinals
5. 1935—Chicago Cubs
6. 1937—St. Louis Cardinals
7. 1938—Cincinnati Reds
8. 1939—Cincinnati Reds
9. 1940—Cincinnati Reds
10. 1941—Brooklyn Dodgers
11. 1942—St. Louis Cardinals
12. 1943,
    1946,
    1948—St. Louis Cardinals
13. 1944—St. Louis Cardinals
14. 1945—Chicago Cubs
15. 1947—Boston Braves
16. 1949—Brooklyn Dodgers
17. 1950—Philadelphia Phillies
18. 1951,
    1953,
    1955—Brooklyn Dodgers
19. 1952—Chicago Cubs
20. 1954,
    1965—New York, San Fran-
    cisco Giants
21. 1956—Brooklyn Dodgers
22. 1957—Milwaukee Braves
23. 1958,
    1959—Chicago Cubs
24. 1960—Pittsburgh Pirates
25. 1961—Cincinnati Reds
26. 1962—Los Angeles Dodgers
27. 1963—Los Angeles Dodgers
28. 1964—St. Louis Cardinals
29. 1966—Pittsburgh Pirates
30. 1967—St. Louis Cardinals
31. 1968—St. Louis Cardinals
32. 1969—San Francisco Giants
33. 1970,
    1972—Cincinnati Reds
34. 1971—St. Louis Cardinals
35. 1973—Cincinnati Reds

```
A F R E I L O B C K O R Q W O R T S J E R O M E D E A N T L V O E S T
F R O K C H A R L E S K L E I N E Q W R N M O K L E A S P L H F G D E
T A L E S T P K R O K L P Q S L T R O L E H L A D B E P E T E R O S E
A N S T R O W E R O K I T V U C L U O T C R E E T E U A N B D A C K L
A K E S T O P Q E L C D R O E A C I K N L E V Q U L H O A T E N S E R
T I N O V E B M O C W E N N O D O T E L C K L M O Q S T R U C K O U V
K E N B O Y E R E L O N C A B O K B L M L O M E O N V E R N E M A A C
T F R C H L K E V Q Z W A T U R Y E S L C K C L I B O L L I N C A R E
C R E K T R O V E R N I E B A N K S E T O C L B V E S W I C K C L D E
R I T A K R A S U E T N L O N T O B E N S O O R T Q U I D H O O L T S
S S L O T P J K C I V S R H A N B T R C K R L V A R N L E Y O R T E N
K C A J K O A P T R E L O H G U Q S E R K I V R E A T L S N O M E R S
M H O V I U K O P T F J G R H O H G E C K M A U R Y W I L L S I T R Q
O D O L U M E A F T U L O L S R E U A V R E L K E B D E A R O C I O L
T E N N Y O K E R P A G R A L H O J C K O P E Z W K O M V O T K S T E
I K E R J A N O A R E A T O C K M C C L V R O K E R O A S Q U W O E R
D A P Q O L K C N D C E V R O Y C A M P A N E L L A Q Y T C A B G O H
R A L L E Y O V K S I J T L E M O N A A N E V Q S L K S E E R O K J O
A P E L M K O M R N T E A V O L A C N L T O G S E R B C L K L G O O D
B E A C E O M E O T K A L V T G B U C K Y W A L T E R S Q A L A N O T
M I T E D W L A B D L K N S O M N E T E E M Q U T G K O A T U B E A R
O T I Q W E V A I L O K S T A N M U S I A L A N N T Q W R T O B T Z L
L E L K I B R A N T O E C U Y L T O E V A P E O T L O T R E A Y B H R
E D L B C A N O S K L N Q Z H D R L R O O M Q R Z O P L T R E H Z A R
I K I C K E M P O K E C B D F E C K O L E T N A W K O V E R A A T N A
N O M L Q C S A N D Y K O U F A X C L L D E T A W N P U Q A E R S K V
R A A E W L E A T H Q E Z T U G A V C E A L S K N G L H V V S T E S T
E D C V N T O N Y A V D I C K G R O A T Q O R N T U N K R A T N O A V
T E H A M D E L P H O V E V D C T K L V O N E A V T O Y Z C W E R U R
H L P L O T V G A T U L K E F R A L C O N V K H A S W X O L C T X E A
O K L E T Q O R L A N D O C E P E D A P P R C D A N X U A I Q T E R D
T B O B E L L I O T W L E B R O X W A N T S B X O V A T L H E A C K E
K O D E Q N E A K E X M O R T C O O P E R T M D B T Q C T P O T T E K
W E R K V C O O P U T R Z X Y O K A D A K T O N S M O W X V R T O E L
T M A R T Y M A R I O N B E R O E W C O O K S N O S B I G B O B N E M
```

16.

ANSWERS

ANSWERS: 1. BASEBALL QUIZ—MULTIPLE CHOICE

1. d. Frank Robinson
2. b. Ted Williams
3. a. .406
4. c. Maury Wills
5. d. 104
6. b. Lou Gehrig
7. c. 2,130
8. b. Stan Musial (5)
9. b. Dale Long (8)
10. b. Bob Gibson (24)
11. a. 37 (Wes Ferrell)
12. c. 0
13. a. 17
14. c. Red Sox
15. d. Joe Nuxhall
16. a. round
17. b. Sandy Koufax
18. c. 565 ft.
19. b. Joe DiMaggio
20. c. 56
21. c. Jim Northrup and Jim Gentile
22. c. Ty Cobb (34)

23. d. Spalding
24. c. Ty Cobb (.367)
25. b. Wrigley Field
26. c. cricket
27. a. 13 (B. Richardson, L. Brock)
28. b. Don Larsen
29. c. 1935
30. c. Yankees
31. b. 90 ft.
32. c. Roger Maris*
33. d. Bob Feller
34. c. Jackie Robinson
35. b. 24
36. a. 6
37. b. Bob Gibson
38. d. Lou Gehrig (23)
39. d. Bruce Kison (3)
40. a. Cardinals (T. Simmons, B. Stinson)
41. c. Smokey Burgess
42. c. Babe Ruth (2,056)
43. d. Ron Hunt (227)
44. c. 1

45. d. Cardinals
46. b. Sal Maglie
47. d. Yankees
48. b. 1929
49. d. 15
50. c. Tony Oliva
51. b. Orlando Cepeda (38)
52. a. Joe Torre (352)
53. d. Jim Hickman
54. a. Tony Cloninger (7/3/66)
55. b. Ron Hansen
56. c. Bobby Wine (137)
57. a. 93
58. b. 1927
59. b. Yogi Berra
60. a. Tony Conigliaro
61. b. Willie Stargell
62. d. 4
63. b. 18
64. d. 37
65. b. Browns
66. c. 32
67. c. Dave McNally
68. a. Phillies and Pirates
69. d. Willie Stargell (.646)
70. b. 124
71. a. Bobby Bonds (148)

72. b. Darrell Evans (124)
73. d. Mike Cuellar
74. a. Cubs
75. b. Frank Robinson (552)
76. c. Max Carey (738)
77. a. 30
78. d. 3 (2 grand slams)
79. b. Donn Clendennon
80. c. 0
81. b. Elston Howard
82. d. Frank Howard
83. a. Mets (.509)
84. b. Braves (.427)
85. d. Mets (.338)
86. d. Ed Kranepool
87. c. Rod Carew
88. b. 32
89. c. 1,552
90. c. Twins
91. d. Indians
92. b. Bill North
93. a. Rod Carew
94. c. 383
95. a. 0
96. a. Nap Lajoie
97. b. Hoyt Wilhelm
98. a. Bobby Murcer (102)

ANSWERS: 2. NICKNAMES

1. Phil Rizzuto
2. George H. "Babe" Ruth
3. Willie Mays
4. Bill Skowron
5. Jim Hunter
6. Ralph Garr
7. George Sternweis
8. Dick Radatz
9. Gene Michaels
10. Willie McCovey
11. Edwin Snider
12. John Baker
13. Lou Gehrig
14. Joe DiMaggio
15. Virgil Trucks
16. Carl Furillo
17. Harold Reese
18. John Milner / Hank Aaron
19. George H. "Babe" Ruth
20. Frank McGraw
21. Charles Stengel
22. Louis Newsom
23. Frankie Frisch
24. Pete Reiser
25. Eddie Lopat
26. Larry Berra
27. Harmon Killebrew
28. Joe Dugan
29. Elwin Roe
30. Allie Reynolds
31. George Theodore
32. Phil Reagan
33. John Martin
34. Frank Howard

35. Enos Slaughter	52. Jacob Buckley
36. Alex Hamner	53. Ernie Lombardi
37. John Powell	54. John McGraw
38. Jim Rhodes	55. Jim Lefebvre
39. Harry Lowry	56. Thurman Munson
40. George Kelly	57. Joe Gordon
41. Paul Waner	58. Dick McAuliffe
42. Lloyd Waner	59. August Galan
43. Harold Traynor	60. Spurgeon Chandler
44. Joe Medwick	61. Glenn Beckert
45. Charlie Keller	62. Willie Comet
46. Ted Williams	63. Sam McDowell
47. Rod Kanael	64. Jim Gentile
48. George Scott	65. Dom DiMaggio
49. Stan Musial	66. Bob Belinsky
50. John Odom	67. Pete Rose
51. Forrest Burgess	68. Wilfred Siebert

69. Sal Maglie

70. Adrian Anson

71. George Selkirk

72. Henry Manush

73. Bob Bailey

74. Leon Goslin

75. Harry Lavagetto

76. Bob Gibson

77. Orlando Cepeda

78. Joe Jackson

79. Wilmer Mizell

80. Ted Kluszewski

81. Wilbert Robinson

82. Don Newcombe

83. Harold Chase

84. Ewell Blackwell

85. Walter Maranville

86. Lucius Appling

87. Frank Lary

88. Bobby Brown

89. Jim Gilliam

90. Lynwood Rowe

91. Lou Novikoff

92. Max Carey

93. Tony Lazzeri

94. John Chesbro

95. Marty Marion

96. Ty Cobb

97. Clint Courtney

98. Johnny Mize

99. Al Simmons

100. Earle Coombs

101. Ken Harrelson

102. Jim Kaat

103. Charles Hartnett	115. Fred Petersen
104. Fred Haney	116. Waite Hoyt
105. Rogers Hornsby	117. Paul Blair
106. Mike Higgins	118. Mordecai Brown
107. Sam Crawford	119. Ellis Kinder
108. Carl Hubbell	120. Harry Brecheen
109. William Hoy	121. Willie Keeler
110. Julian Javier	122. Jesse Burkett
111. Garry Maddox	123. Willie Horton
112. Fred Hutchinson	124. Don Hoak
113. Ron Hunt	125. Americo Petrocelli
114. Johnny Bench	126. Jesse Haines

ANSWERS: 3. BALLPARKS

1. Wrigley Field

2. Metropolitan Stadium

3. Atlanta Stadium

4. Jarry Park

5. Riverfront Stadium

6. Candlestick Park

7. Shea Stadium

8. Fenway Park

9. Veterans Stadium

10. Memorial Stadium

11. Three Rivers Stadium

12. Busch Stadium

13. Anaheim Stadium

14. Cleveland Stadium

15. Arlington Stadium

ANSWERS: 4. BASEBALL QUIZ

1. Walter Holke (42 putouts, 43 chances—26-inning game)
2. Rogers Hornsby (1922 and 1925)
3. 6
4. 24 (V. Davalillo, Cardinals, 1970; D. Philley, Orioles, 1961)
5. No (1 pinch hit per game per player)
6. Boston Red Sox (7/30/36, St. Louis to Chicago)
7. 11 (Aaron, Anson, Clemente, Cobb, E. Collins, Lajoie, Mays, Musial, Speaker, P. Waner, and H. Wagner)
8. Ted Williams (age 39)
9. Casey Stengel (1962)
10. Philadelphia Athletics (56 players in 1915)
11. 26 innings (Braves v. Dodgers; 5/1/20; Braves 2, Dodgers 1)
12. 1908
13. Connie Mack
14. Nen, Kazak, Harrah, Hannah
15. A pitcher who can work often
16. Tom Egan (7/28/70, Angels)
17. Frank Howard (5/12 to 5/18/68; 10 homeruns in 20 at bats)
18. 14
19. Barney McCoskey (Philadelphia Athletics)
20. Hank Majeski (6, Philadelphia Athletics, 8/27/48)
21. There is none.
22. Bruno Haas (Philadelphia Athletics, 1915)
23. Bob Robertson (Pirates, 10/3/71)
24. Bill Melton (33 home runs, 1970)
25. Don Kessinger (6/17/71)
26. Hank Aaron
27. Grover Cleveland Alexander
28. Hank Aaron (6, 424)
29. Joe Adcock (18)
30. 4 home runs, 1 double (18)
31. 118
32. 123
33. 4 times (1956, 1957, 1958, 1959)

34. Pirates (56 innings, 6/1 to 6/9/03)
35. Don Drysdale (6: 5/14, 5/18, 5/22, 5/26, 5/31, and 6/4/68)
36. Roger Craig (1962)
37. Johnny Allen (15-1 in 1937, .938)
38. 8 (Walter Hines, Boston Braves, 1937)
39. 30 (AL players–13, NL players–17)
40. a. Jesse C. Burkett: 1895–1896 (.409, .410), Indians
    b. Ty Cobb: 1911–1912 (.420, .410), Tigers
    c. Rogers Hornsby: 1924–1925 (.424, .403), Cardinals
41. Bobby Byrne (12, 11 innings, 6/8/10)
42. Ray Chapman (Indians, 1920; Pitcher: Carl Mays, Yankees)
43. 22 (Tom Jones, Browns; Hal Chase, Yankees; Ernie Banks, Cubs)
44. Charles A. Comiskey
45. Jack Coombs (13, Philadelphia Athletics, 1910)
46. 14 (Thomas Corcoran, Reds, 1903)
47. Sam "Wahoo" Crawford (309)
48. Luis Aparacio (7,612)
49. Hack Wilson (190, Cubs, 1930)
50. Babe Ruth (2,209)
51. Leo "Lippy" Durocher
52. Tommy Holmes (37 games, Boston Braves, 1945)
53. George Stone (Mets, 12–3, .800)
54. 29 (Victor Willis, Boston Braves, 1905)
55. 2
56. 352
57. Earned runs $\times$ 9 $\div$ innings $=$ ERA
58. Willard Schmidt (Reds, 4/26/59)
59. 4 (Chet Ross, Red Sox, 5/17/25)
60. Between 5 and 5¼ ozs.
61. Bill Holbert (2,335 at bats, 1876–1888)
62. Carl Yastrzemski
63. Willie Mays
64. 6
65. 3
66. Wally Pipp

67. Babe Dahlgren
68. 4 (Achieved by many)
69. 6 (6 walks, Jimmy Foxx, Red Sox, 6/16/38)
70. Lou Gehrig
71. a. Lloyd Waner (198, Pirates, 1927)
    b. Earl Webb (67, Red Sox, 1931)
    c. J. Owen Wilson (36, Pirates, 1912)
72. Matty Alou (698, Pirates, 1969)
73. Hal Lanier (.239, 1968)
74. Hank Aaron (14)
75. Willie Mays (13)
76. Ty Cobb (3,033)
77. 2,244 (Ty Cobb)
78. 11 (Achieved by many)
79. George Sisler (257 for St. Louis, 1920)
80. 1962
81. William "Sliding Billy" Hamilton (24)
82. 11; Willie Horton, Tigers, 7/18/69.
83. Franklin Hayes (29, Indians and Phillies, 1945)
84. 7 (Guy Hecker, 8/15/86)
85. Paul Hines (1878, Providence, NL)
86. 3 (Achieved by many)
87. Hank Aaron (15)
88. Hank Aaron (1,395 extra base hits: 715 homers, 96 triples, 584 doubles) as of 4/8/74
89. Tris Speaker (793)
90. a. AL: 12 (Bob Cerv, Yankees and K.C. A's)
    b. NL: 18 (Jerry Lynch, Pirates and Reds)
91. Ralph Kiner (7 seasons: 1947–1952)
92. a. AL: Hank Greenberg (39 homers—1938)
    b. NL: Ted Kluszewski (34 homers—1954)
93. a. AL: Babe Ruth (32 homers—1927)
    b. NL: Eddie Matthews (30 homers—1953)
94. Mickey Mantle (10)

95. Phil Rizzuto (1949–1952)
96. a. AL: Russ Nixon (3, Red Sox, 1965)
    b. NL: Ernie Banks (3, Cubs, 1961)
97. Ted Williams (1946–1949)
98. a. Hank Aaron (283, Braves)
    b. Frank Robinson (4, Reds, 1961–1964)
    c. Willie McCovey (45, Giants, 1969)
99. a. AL: Jackie Jensen (3, Red Sox: 1954, 1956, 1957)
    b. NL: Ernie Lombardi (4, Reds: 1933, 1934, 1938, and Giants: 1944)
100. Ted Williams (145 in 1939)
101. a. AL: George Scott (152, Red Sox, 1966)
     b. NL: Larry Hisle (152, Phillies, 1969)
102. Eddie Sawyer
103. a. Cy Young: Tom Seaver
     b. MVP: Pete Rose
104. a. Cy Young: Jim Palmer
     b. MVP: Reggie Jackson
105. Rico Petrocelli (40, Red Sox, 1969)
106. 7 (Vic Raschi, 8/4/53)
107. Charlie Root (1932)
108. Charles "Red" Ruffing
109. 6
110. a. Hank Greenberg (1935)
     b. Al Rosen (1953)
     c. Mickey Mantle (1956)
     d. Frank Robinson (1966)
     e. Denny McClain (1968)
     f. Reggie Jackson (1973)
111. 6
112. a. Lefty Grove (1931)
     b. Spud Chandler (1943)
     c. Hal Newhouser (1944–1945)
     d. Bobby Shantz (1952)
     e. Denny McClain (1968)
     f. Vida Blue (1971)

113. Bert Campaneris and Cesar Tovar
114. Babe Ruth (.690)
115. 1846–1887
116. Willie Stargell (44 homers, 119 RBI's)
117. Mike Marshall (92, Expo's, 1973)
118. 335
119. 7; 13
120. 8; 38
121. 115 (Roger Maris: 61; Mickey Mantle: 54)
122. Ralph Kiner (Pirates); Johnny Mize (Giants)
123. Tom Zachary (Senators, 9/30/27)
124. Tracy Stallard (Red Sox, 10/1/61)
125. 10 (5/1, 5/31, 6/11, 6/22, 7/9, 7/26, 9/6, 9/7, 9/13, 9/29/27)
126. 8 (5/30, 6/11, 7/2, 7/25 (dble. hdr.) 8/13, 8/16, 9/2/61)
127. 223
128. 54
129. 4; Goose Goslin (Tigers, 4/28/34), Mike Kreevich (White Sox, 8/4/39)
130. Eddie Yost
131. 18
132. Jim Wynn (148, Astro's, 1969)
133. Billy Williams (1,117, Cubs, 1963–1970)
134. Vic Wertz (Indians)
135. John Warhop (6/6/15, Yankees)
136. Matty Alou (.342) and Felipe Alou (.327) in 1966
137. Luke Appling
138. Richie Ashburn (1948)
139. Cornelius "Neal" Ball (Indians, 7/19/09, against Red Sox)
140. 2,528
141. Eephus pitch
142. Bo Belinsky (5/5/62)
143. Johnny Bench (154, Reds, 1968)
144. Al Kaline (age 20; .340, Tigers, 1955)
145. Wee Willie Keeler and John McGraw (Orioles, 1890s)

146. 44 (Wee Willie Keeler, Orioles, 1897)
147. 8 (NL: George "High Pockets" Kelly, 6/14/24, Giants)
     (AL: Robert Johnson, 6/12/38, Athletics)
148. Michael J. "King" Kelly
149. Forbes Field
150. 5
151. Bobby Bonds (for Giants v. Dodgers, 6/25/68)
152. Lou Boudreau (24 years old)
153. Roger "Duke" Bresnahan (1908)
154. Chick Hafey (.3489), Bill Terry (.3486), Jim Bottomley (.3482)
155. 1936
156. Ty Cobb, Honus Wagner, and Christy Matthewson
157. Napoleon Lajoie (.422, Philadelphia Athletics, 1901)
158. Rudy York (5/16, 5/22, and 5/30/38)
159. Jim Lemon (8/31/56, against Whitey Ford)
160. Whitey Lockman
161. 6. (Many achieved this feat)
162. Al Lopez (1,918)
163. Sammy Byrd
164. Forest "Hick" Cady
165. AL: Rod Carew (7, Twins, 1969)
     NL: Pete Reiser (7, Dodgers, 1946)
166. 19 (Steve Carlton, 9/15/69; Tom Seaver, 4/22/70)
167. 6 (Achieved by many)
168. Dean Chance (63, Twins, 1968)
169. Horace Clark (Yankees)
170. Yes (Jack Clements and Dale Long)
171. 9 (Tony Cloninger, Milwaukee Braves, 7/3/66)
172. Nate Colbert (13, Padres, 8/1/72—5 homers, 2 singles)

173. Thomas Henry Connally (AL) and Bill Klem (NL)
174. Giants (1964–1965)
175. Jim Manning
176. Roy Foster (12)
177. Morgan Bulkeley (1876)
178. Joe Schultz
179. Joe Morgan (122, Reds)
180. Terry Harmon (18, Phillies, 6/12/71)
181. Jack Aker (Kansas City A's)
182. 25 (Reds v. Cubs, 10/8/00)
183. Robinson Field
184. Fred Thayer
185. Minnie Minoso (189)
186. 2-¾ in.
187. 308
188. White Sox (3, 1908)
189. 30 (Tigers v. Philadelphia Athletics, 5/19/16)
190. 1876
191. 20 (Yankees, v. Red Sox, 9/21/56)
192. Larry Dierker (in W-20, L-13; 1969)
193. Dick Dietz (25, Giants)
194. Dom DiMaggio (31, 1949)
195. Larry Doby (Indians, 7/3/47)
196. John "Dirty Jack" Doyle (6/7/92)
197. AL: Washington Senators—288 (1913)
     NL: N.Y. Giants—347 (1911)
198. 503 (Dom DiMaggio, Red Sox, 1948)
199. Crosley Field (Cincinnati)
200. Juan Marichal (W-238, L-140)
201. The Green Monster (315 ft. from home plate, 37 ft. high)
202. 5 (Ernie Banks, Ray Walls, Dale Long, Walt Moryn, Bobby Thompson)
203. 516 (Dom DiMaggio, Red Sox, 1948)

204. Jack Fisher, Steve Barber, Chuck Estrada, Jerry Walker, Milt Pappas
205. Al "Rube" Walker
206. 56 (Trucks: 27; Newhouser: 29)
207. 31
208. Mickey Vernon (2,227)
209. Eddie Gael (St. Louis Brown, 3 ft.7 in.); Uniform No: ⅛
210. Honus Wagner (676)
211. George "Specs" Topercer (Cardinals, 1921)
212. Bill Terry (.401, Giants, 1930)
213. New York Giants (1913)
214. Bob Tolan (57)
215. Bob Tillman (17)
216. Sam "Big Sam" Thompson (126)
217. Hank Thompson (43)
218. John Taylor (352, Cardinals, 1904)
219. Chuck Tanner (White Sox)
220. 1
221. 1913
222. Nap Rucker (Score: Dodgers 3, Giants 2)
223. 138 (Johnny Edwards, Astro's)
224. Ken Keltner
225. Russell Blackburne (White Sox)
226. Ron Santo (rejected trade to Angels, went to White Sox)
227. Stan Musial (1943, 1946, 1948) and Roy Campanella (1951, 1953, 1955)
228. Orlando Cepeda
229. Ernie Banks (1958–1959)
230. 2 (Many accomplished this feat)
231. 1965
232. Rod Carew (.318, Twins, 1972)
233. Lou Chizza, May 24, 1935 (Crosley Field)
234. Highlanders
235. John Frederick (6, Dodgers, 1932)
236. Mickey Mantle (Yankees) and Whitey Ford (Yankees)

237. Jim Fregosi
238. Peter Gray
239. Frank Robinson (552)
240. 3 (George Burnside, Washington Senators; Jim Perry, Indians; Frank Lary, Tigers)
241. 24; Mets v. Astro's (4/15/68; score: Astro's 1, Mets 0)
242. Hank Greenberg (1947, Pirates; left Tigers after 1946)
243. Jerry Grote (24-inning game, v. Astro's, 4/15/68)
244. Reggie Jackson (1968: 171; 1969: 142; 1970: 135; 1971: 161)
245. Cubs: Hank Sauer; Pirates: Ralph Kiner
246. Giants: Willie McCovey; Braves: Hank Aaron
247. Red Sox: Carl Yastrzemski; Twins: Harmon Killebrew
248. Dom DiMaggio; 15
249. 2 (1947: 39; 1949: 37)
250. Max Carey (Pirates); 62
251. Had smallest feet in ML's (left ft., size 4½; right ft., size 4)
252. Astro's: Cesar Cedeno; Phillies: Willie Montanez
253. A's: Amos Otis; Twins: Tony Oliva and Cesar Tovar
254. Cubs: Billy Williams; Reds: Pete Rose
255. Billy Herman (16, Cubs, 6/28/33)
256. Ted Williams
257. 2 (Achieved by many)
258. With a runner on second, he hit line drive that bounced off pitcher's head and was caught in the air by catcher, who threw to second base to double up runner.
259. Gil Hodges
260. Tommy Holmes (1945, Boston Braves—28 home runs, 9 strikeouts, 636 at bats)
261. Burt Hooton (4/16/72 v. Phillies)
262. Forfeit
263. Frank Howard (10)
264. .643
265. 502

266. Atlanta Braves (Hank Aaron, Darrell Evans, and Dave Johnson; 1973)
267. AL: Dick Allen (White Sox); NL: Willie Stargell (Pirates)
268. Ron Hunt (24)
269. Harmon Killebrew (48, 45, and 49 home runs respectively)
270. 49 (Rollie "Bunions" Zeider, White Sox, 1910)
271. Royce Youngs (Giants, 1917–1926)
272. Eddie Yost (2,356; Senators, Tigers, and Angels)
273. Fred Snodgrass (Giants v. Red Sox)
274. Red Rolfe
275. Arthur Irwin (1883)
276. St. Louis Browns
277. Byron (Ban) Johnson
278. Cleon Jones (26)
279. White Sox
280. George Kell
281. AL: Indians (111, 1954); NL: Cubs (116, 1906)
282. A's, Padres, and Indians
283. Ivey Wingo (234, Cardinals and Reds, 1911–1929)
284. Charles Sweezy (Reds, 1869)
285. Ernest Swanson (13.3 sec., Reds and White Sox, 1929)
286. Chuck Stobbs
287. Harry Stovey (1880–1893)
288. Glen Stephens
289. Dick Sisler
290. Charlie Silvera
291. Burt Shotten
292. Glen Stephens (Red Sox—on 6/18/53 hit a double and 2 singles)
293. Harry Steinfeldt
294. George Sisler (41, Browns, 1922)
295. Tommy Harper (54, Red Sox)
296. Orioles: Al Bumbry; Twins: Rod Carew
297. George Stainback
298. George Selkirk
299. Gil McDougald

300. Carl Sheib (16 yrs., 8 mos., 5 days in 1943)
301. Al Schacht
302. Dominic Ryba (Cardinals and Red Sox, 1935–1946)
303. John Roseboro
304. 1954
305. Eddie Matthews (for Braves v. Dodgers, 9/27/52)
306. Leon Cadore (13, Braves, v. Dodgers, 5/1/20, 26 innings)
307. 3
308. 50 ft.
309. Fred Clark (Louisville, NL, 1894)
310. Sam Crawford (Reds, 1901; Tigers, 1908)
311. Lou Gehrig (184, 1931)
312. Hack Wilson (1929–1930, Cubs)
313. Ned Williams (5/30/84)
314. Ken Williams (4/22/22)
315. Wally Schang (6, Philadelphia Athletics, 5/12/20)
316. Babe Ruth (AL: Yankees; NL: Braves)
317. Red Rolfe (18, Yankees, 1939)
318. Ted Kluszewski (17, Reds, 1954)
319. Tip O'Neill (St. Louis Browns, AA, 1887)
320. Billy Sullivan (1899–1916)
321. Al Simmons (253, Philadelphia Athletics, 1925)
322. Bobby Lowe (Boston—5/30/94)
323. 511—Clyde Milan (Washington Senators, 1910–1913)
324. Roscoe Barnes (5/2/76)
325. Tigers (against Red Sox—both days)
326. Babe Ruth (4/18/23)
327. Fifty cents
328. 125
329. 4/18/23 (Yankees v. Red Sox)
330. Whitey Witt
331. Bob Shawkey

332. 1. Frankie Frisch (1931)
    2. Jerome "Dizzy" Dean (1934)
    3. Joe Medwick (1937)
    4. Mort Cooper (1942)
    5. Stan Musial (1943, 1946, 1948)
    6. Marty Marion (1945)
    7. Ken Boyer (1964)
    8. Orlando Cepeda (1967)
    9. Bob Gibson (1968)
   10. Joe Torre (1971)

333. 1. Lou Gehrig (1936)
    2. Joe DiMaggio (1939, 1941, 1947)
    3. Joe Gordon (1942)
    4. Spud Chandler (1943)
    5. Phil Rizzuto (1950)
    6. Yogi Berra (1951, 1954, 1955)
    7. Mickey Mantle (1956, 1957, 1962)
    8. Roger Maris (1960, 1961)
    9. Elston Howard (1963)

334. Hit into double play with bases loaded (7/18/41 v. Indians)

335. 59

336. Yankees 1, Red Sox 0

337. Plate Appearances: Ruth—692
                        Maris—698
     Official "At Bats": Ruth—540
                        Maris—590

338. 5

339. Thurman Munson (Yankees, 1970)

340. Johnny Bench, (Reds, 1968)

341. East: Orioles; West: A's

342. East: Mets; West: Reds

343. 4/22/76 (Phillies v. Boston Braves)

344. Phillies (1907; Giants lost game when fans started throwing snowballs at players)

345. Reds

346. Jim Hickman (13: 3 home runs, 1 single; 9/3/65)

347. Willie Mays (1955)

ANSWERS: 5. PITCHING QUIZ

1. 4 (1962, 1963, 1964, 1965)

2. 3 no-hitters (1940, 1946, 1951); 11 1-hitters (1936, 1941, 1945, 1956)

3. Johnny Vander Meer (Reds: 6/11/38 v. Braves, 6/15/38 v. Dodgers)
   Allie Reynolds (Yankees: 7/12/51 v. Indians, 9/28/51 v. Red Sox)
   Virgil Trucks (Tigers: 5/15/52 v. Senators, 8/25/52 v. Yankees)
   Nolan Ryan (Angels: 5/15/73 v. Royals, 7/15/73 v. Tigers)

4. Cy Young (Red Sox: 5/5/04 v. Philadelphia Athletics)
   Adrian Joss (Indians: 10/2/08 v. White Sox)
   Charles Robertson (White Sox: 4/30/22 v. Tigers)
   Jim Bunning (Phillies: 6/21/64 v. Mets)
   Sandy Koufax (Dodgers: 9/9/65 v. Cubs)
   Jim Hunter (A's: 8/8/68 v. Twins)

5. Harvey Haddix (Pirates; 5/26/59; Braves 1, Pirates 0)

6. 2 (Claude Passeau: Phillies—1938, Cubs—1945; Jim Carleton: Cubs—1935, Dodgers—1940)

7. Elroy Face (.947: W18–L1 in 1959)

8. Fork ball

9. 511

10. AL: Walter Johnson (Senators, 1913–1916)
    NL: Warren Spahn (Braves, 1957–1961)

11. Robin Roberts (4, Phillies, 1952–1955)

12. Hoyt Wilhelm (651)

13. Elroy Face (574)

14. AL: Red Ruffing (1,833)
    NL: Warren Spahn (1,798)

15. AL: Lou "Bobo" Newsom (186, Browns, 1938)
    NL: Guy Bush (155, Cubs, 1930)

16. AL: 13 (Frank O'Doul—Red Sox)
    NL: 12 (Harold Kelleher—Phillies)

17. AL: Vic Raschi (4, Yankees: 5/3/50 v. White Sox)
    NL: Bob Shaw (5, Braves: 5/4/63 v. Cubs)

18. AL: J. Joseph Boehling (6, Senators, 1915); Vic Raschi (6, Yankees, 1950)
    NL: Bob Shaw (8, Braves, 1963)

19. Walter Johnson (4, Senators, 9/21/14—4th inning)

20. AL: Charles Wheatley (5, Tigers, 9/27/12)
    NL: Laurance Cheney (5, Dodgers, 7/9/18)

21. AL: 156 (Walter Johnson—Senators)
    NL: 156 (Leon Ames—Giants, Reds, Cardinals, Phillies)

22. AL: Bob Feller (208, Indians, 1938)
    NL: Samuel Jones (185, Cubs, 1955)

23. Tommy Byrne (16, Browns, 13-inning game, 8/22/51)

24. Steve Carlton (Phillies, 1972)

25. Ron Swoboda (Score: Mets 4, Phillies 2)

26. Alva "Bobo" Holloman (Browns, 5/7/53)

27. Don Sutton (9, Dodgers)

28. Albert Spalding (1871–1878, Boston, Nat'l Assoc, and Cubs, NL)

29. Nolan Ryan (Angels)

30. Leon Cadore (5/1/20)

31. George "Zip" Zabel (Cubs, 18⅓ innings, 6/17/15)

32. Ed Summers (Tigers, 18-inning tie game, 6/16/09)

33. 464 (Ed Walsh, White Sox, 1908)

34. Bert Blyleven (9, Twins)

35. 4

36. Nolan Ryan (2, Angels), Steve Busby (1, Royals), Jim Bibby (1, Rangers)

37. 11

38. Jim Palmer (Orioles)   Ken Holtzman (A's)
    Wilbur Wood (White Sox)   Bill Singer (Angels)
    Jim Hunter (A's)   Paul Splittorf (Royals)
    Joe Coleman (Tigers)   Jim Colborn (Brewers)
    Luis Tiant (Red Sox)   Bert Blyleven (Twins)
    Vida Blue (A's)

39. John Hiller (38, Tigers)

40. Gaylord Perry (29, Indians)

41. Wilbur Wood (48, White Sox)

42. Steve Busby (Royals) and Jim Bibby (Rangers)

43. Wilbur Wood (359⅓ innings pitched, 166 runs allowed, 381 hits allowed)

44. Ron Bryant (24, Giants)

45. Wilbur Wood (24, White Sox)

46. Jack Chesbro (48, Yankees, 1904)

47. Victor Willis (45, Boston Braves, 1902)

48. 16 (1 NL, 3 AL pitchers); Harold Kelleher (Phillies, 5/5/38, 8th inning)

49. Ray Narleski (4)

50. Elroy Face (8)

51. Ned Garver (9). (Milt Pappas also allowed 9, but 6 AL and 3 NL)

52. Walter Johnson (4,920, Senators, 1907–1927)

53. Grover Cleveland Alexander (4,868, Phillies, Cubs, Cardinals, 1911–1930)

54. Early Wynn (335, Senators, Indians, White Sox, 1939–1963)

55. Warren Spahn (434, Braves, Mets, Giants, 1942, 1946–1965)

56. Pedro Ramos (43)

57. Robin Roberts (46)

58. Walter Johnson (204)

59. Don Drysdale (154)

60. Dick Radatz (16, Red Sox, 1964)

61. Elroy Face (18, Pirates, 1959)

ANSWERS: 6. ALL-STAR GAME QUIZ

1. 0

2. 4 (1959–1962)

3. Comiskey Park (1933)

4. AL (Score: AL 4, NL 2)

5. Winner: Lefty Gomez (Yankees); Loser: Bill Hallahan (Cardinals)

6. AL: Connie Mack (Philadelphia Athletics); NL: John McGraw (Giants)

7. AL: Babe Ruth (Yankees); NL: Frankie Frisch (Cardinals)

8. Stan Musial (24, Cardinals)

9. Ted Williams (10, Red Sox, 1946)

10. Carl Yastrzemski (1970—12 innings, Red Sox)

11. Joe "Arky" Vaughn—Pirates (1941)
    Ted Williams—Red Sox (1946)
    Al Rosen—Indians (1954)
    Willie McCovey—Giants (1969)

12. 5 (Ted Williams, Red Sox, 1946; Al Rosen, Indians, 1954)

13. Roberto Clemente (4, Pirates, 1967—15 innings)

14. Mickey Mantle (17, Yankees)

15. Willie Mays (20, Giants)

16. AL: Charlie Gehringer (1934)
    NL: Phil Cavarretta (1944)

17. AL: Lefty Gomez (6, Yankees, 1934)
    NL: Larry Jansen (5, Giants, 1950)

18. 5 (Claude Passeau, Cubs, 1941;
       Jim Maloney, Reds, 1965;
       Sandy Consuegra, White Sox, 1954)

19. Carl Hubbell (5, 1934—Ruth, Gehrig, Foxx, Simmins, Cronin)

20. Charlie Gehringer (.500, Tigers)

21. AL: Early Wynn (6, Indians, 1955–1959)
    NL: Ewell Blackwell (6, Reds, 1946–1951)

22. Don Drysdale—(19, Dodgers)

23. Bob Feller (13, Indians)

24. AL: Lefty Gomez (18, Yankees)
    NL: Don Drysdale (19⅓, Dodgers)

25. AL: Whitey Ford (11, Yankees)
    NL: Robin Roberts (10, Phillies)

26. AL: Whitey Ford (19, Yankees)
    NL: Robin Roberts (17, Phillies) and Warren Spahn (17, Braves)

27. AL: Jim Brewer, Red Sox
    NL: Robin Roberts, Phillies;   Juan Marichal, Giants;   Ewell
        Blackwell, Reds

28. Early Wynn (AL, 3, 1957—5th inning)

29. 1945

30. Willie Mays (game: 2; lifetime: 6)

31. Tony Oliva (2, Twins)

32. AL: Ted Williams (10, Red Sox)
    NL: Willie Mays (16, Giants)

33. AL: Brooks Robinson (13, Orioles)
    NL: Stan Musial (10, Cardinals)

34. AL: Ted Williams (14, Red Sox) and Jimmy Foxx (14, Red Sox)
    NL: Willie Mays (23, Giants)

35. AL: Ted Williams (Red Sox, 1946) and Carl Yastrzemski (Red
        Sox, 1970–12 innings)
    NL: Joe Medwick (1937, Cardinals)

36. Willie Mays (13, Giants)

37. Hank Aaron (19, Braves, 1955–1973)

38. 7 (Wally Jones, Phillies, 1950—14 innings)

39. Vida Blue (A's)

40. Carlton Fiske (Red Sox)

41. Jim Hickman (Cubs)

42. Ted Williams (Red Sox, 1946)

43. Frank Sullivan (Red Sox)

44. Gene Conley (Milwaukee Braves)

45. Bob Rush (Cubs, 5 innings—Score: NL 3, AL 2)

46. Bob Lemon (Indians)

1. Once (1904)

2. William Dineen (Red Sox; W-3, L-1)

3. Tigers (1968)

4. Yogi Berra (Yankees)

5. 18

6. 14 (1947, 1949–1953, 1955–1958, 1960–1963)

7. 3: (Tigers v. Cubs, 1907, 12 innings, Score: 3–3)
   (Giants v. Red Sox, 1912, 11 innings, Score: 6–6)
   (Giants v. Yankees, 1922, 10 innings, Score: 3–3)

8. Yankees (29)

9. Phillies (2, games won: 1, games lost: 8)
   S.F. Giants (1, games won: 3, games lost: 4)
   Twins (1, games won: 3, games lost: 4)
   Browns (1, games won: 2, games lost: 4)

10. 746 (Yankees)

11. Won 20, Lost 9

12. a. 4-game WS: 2 (Deal, Braves, 1914; Maranville, Braves, 1914)
    b. 5-game WS: 6 (Slagle, Cubs, 1907)
    c. 6-game WS: 3 (Collins, White Sox, 1917)
    d. 7-game WS: 7 (Brock, Cardinals, 1967 and 1968)

13. 22 (Yankees v. Giants, 1936)

14. 14 (Yankees v. Giants, 1936)

15. 18 (Yankees, 1936)

16. Yankees (702)

17. 11 (Philadelphia Athletics v. White Sox, 1929;
    Dodgers v. Yankees, 1956)

18. a. 4-game WS: Gehrig (9, Yankees, 1928)
    b. 5-game WS: Murphy (8, Athletics, 1910)
       May (8, Reds, 1970)
    c. 6-game WS: Kluszewski (10, White Sox, 1959)
    d. 7-game WS: Richardson (12, Yankees, 1960)

19. 21 (Yankees v. Giants, 1936;
    Dodgers v. Yankees, 1956)

20. 10 (Athletics v. White Sox, 1929—7th inning;
    Tigers v. Cardinals, 1968—3rd inning)

21. 1,374 (Yankees)

22. 32 (Yankees v. Pirates, 1960)

23. 32 (Yankees, 1928 and 1932)

24. 47 (Yankees v. Dodgers, 1953)

25. 21 (Athletics v. Cubs, 1929—7th inning)

26. Red Sox (3, 1967—4th inning)

27. Yogi Berra (71)

28. Giants (20, v. Yankees, 1921)
    Cardinals (20, v. Red Sox, 1946)

29. 10 (Athletics, v. Cubs, 1929)

30. 6 (Cubs, v. Tigers, 1908)

31. a. 4-game WS: Babe Ruth (10, Yankees, 1938)
    b. 5-game WS: Home Run Baker (9, Athletics, 1910 and 1913)
                  Ed Collins (9, Athletics, 1910)
                  Heinie Groh (9, Giants 1922)
                  Terry Moore (9, Giants 1937)
                  Bobby Richardson (9, Yankees, 1961)
                  Paul Blair (9, Orioles 1970)
                  Brooks Robinson (9, Orioles, 1970)
    c. 6-game WS: Billy Martin (12, Yankees, 1953)
    d. 7-game WS: Bobby Richardson (13, Yankees, 1964)
                  Lou Brock (13, Cardinals, 1968)

32. a. 4-game WS: Lou Gehrig (.727, Yankees, 1928)
    b. 5-game WS: Joe Gordon (.929, Yankees, 1941)
    c. 6-game WS: Babe Ruth (1.000, Yankees, 1923)
    d. 7-game WS: Gene Tenace (.913, A's, 1972)

33. a. 4-game WS: Babe Ruth (22, Yankees, 1928)
    b. 5-game WS: Brooks Robinson (17, Orioles, 1970)
    c. 6-game WS: Billy Martin (23, Yankees, 1953)
    d. 7-game WS: Duke Snider (24, Dodgers, 1952)
                  Lou Brock (24, Cardinals, 1968)

34. a. 4-game WS: Lou Gehrig (4, Yankees, 1928)
    b. 5-game WS: Donn Clendenon (3, Mets, 1969)
    c. 6-game WS: Babe Ruth (3, Yankees, 1923)
                  Ted Kluszewski (3, Reds, 1959)
    d. 7-game WS: Babe Ruth (4, Yankees, 1926)
                  Duke Snider (4, Dodgers, 1952)
                  Hank Bauer (4, Yankees, 1958)
                  Gene Tenace (4, A's, 1972)

35. a. 4-game WS: Bobby Thompson (7, Giants, 1954)
    b. 5-game WS: Jimmy Sheekard (7, Cubs, 1910)
                  Mickey Cochrane (7, Athletics, 1929)
                  Joe Gordon (7, Yankees, 1941)
    c. 6-game WS: Babe Ruth (8, Yankees, 1923)
    d. 7-game WS: Babe Ruth (11, Yankees, 1926)

36. a. 4-game WS: Babe Ruth (.625, Yankees, 1928)
    b. 5-game WS: Joe Gordon (.500, Yankees, 1941)
                  John McLean (.500, Yankees, 1913)
    c. 6-game WS: Billy Martin (.500, Yankees, 1953)
                  Davis Robertson (.500, Giants, 1917)
    d. 7-game WS: Pepper Martin (.500, Cardinals, 1931)

37. a. 4-game WS: Bob Meusel (7, Yankees, 1927)
    b. 5-game WS: Rogers Hornsby (8, Cubs, 1929)
                  Duke Snider (8, Dodgers, 1949)
    c. 6-game WS: Jim Bottomly (9, Cardinals, 1930)
    d. 7-game WS: Eddie Matthews (11, Braves, 1958)

38. 49

39. Al Weiss (batted .455 in WS)

40. Elmer Smith (Indians, v. Dodgers, 1920)

41. Hank Bauer

42. Cookie Lavagetto (double; Score: Dodgers 3, Yankees 2)

43. Joe Black (Dodgers v. Yankees on 10/1/52)

44. Harry "The Cat" Brecheen (Cardinals, v. Red Sox, 1946)

45. Mickey Owen (Dodgers, v. Yankees)

46. .362

47. 2 (Achieved by many; last: Tommy Davis, Dodgers, 10/3/63)

48. Willie Davis (3, Dodgers, v. Orioles, 10/11/65—5th inning)

49. Pitcher: Hugh Casey (Dodgers)
    Batter: Tommy Henrich (Yankees)
    Count: 3 balls, 2 strikes

50. Bill Wambsganss (1920 WS, 5th game—Indians v. Dodgers)

51. Bill Mazeroski

52. 9

53. Fred Clarke (for Pirates, v. Red Sox)

54. 29⅔ innings (1916, 1918)

55. Frankie Frisch, (1921–1924: .300, .471, .400, .333)

56. Whitey Ford (33⅔ innings)

57. Chuck Hiller (Giants, v. Yankees, 1962 WS—fourth game)

58. Claude Passeau, Hank Borowy, Paul Derringer, Henry "Hoos"
    Wyse

59. Dizzy and Daffy Dean (Cardinals, v. Tigers)

60. Casey Stengel (Giants, v. Yankees)

61. Christy Matthewson (Giants, v. A's)

62. Black Sox Scandal

63. Casey Stengel (Giants, v. Yankees, 10/10/23, inside-the-park
    homerun)

64. Willie Mays (Giants, v. Yankees)

65. Dale Mitchell (pinch hitter); struck out—called 3rd strike

ANSWERS: 8. ROOKIE-OF-THE-YEAR QUIZ

AL	NL
1. 1949—Roy Sievers	1. 1949—Don Newcombe
2. 1950—Walt Dropo	2. 1950—Sam Jethroe
3. 1951—Gil McDougald	3. 1951—Willie Mays
4. 1952—Harry Byrd	4. 1952—Joe Black
5. 1953—Harvey Kuenn	5. 1953—Junior Gilliam
6. 1954—Bob Grim	6. 1954—Wally Moon
7. 1955—Herb Score	7. 1955—Bill Virdon
8. 1956—Luis Aparicio	8. 1956—Frank Robinson
9. 1957—Tony Kubek	9. 1957—Jack Sanford
10. 1958—Albie Pearson	10. 1958—Orlando Cepeda
11. 1959—Bob Allison	11. 1959—Willie McCovey
12. 1960—Ron Hansen	12. 1960—Frank Howard
13. 1961—Don Schwall	13. 1961—Billy Williams
14. 1962—Tom Tresh	14. 1962—Ken Hubbs
15. 1963—Gary Peters	15. 1963—Pete Rose
16. 1964—Tony Oliva	16. 1964—Richie Allen
17. 1965—Curt Blefary	17. 1965—Jim Lefebvre
18. 1966—Tommie Agee	18. 1966—Tommy Helms
19. 1967—Rod Carew	19. 1967—Tom Seaver
20. 1968—Stan Bahnsen	20. 1968—Johnny Bench
21. 1969—Lou Piniella	21. 1969—Ted Sizemore
22. 1970—Thurman Munson	22. 1970—Carl Morton
23. 1971—Chris Chambliss	23. 1971—Earl Williams
24. 1972—Carlton Fiske	24. 1972—Jon Matlack
25. 1973—Al Bumbry	25. 1973—Gary Matthews

ANSWERS: 9. HOME RUN LEADERS BY POSITION—SEASON AND LIFETIME

AL—SEASON

Pitcher: Wes Ferrell (Indians, 1931)
Catcher: Yogi Berra (Yankees, 1956); Gus Triandos (Orioles, 1958)
First Base: Hank Greenberg (Tigers, 1938)
Second Base: Joe Gordon (Indians, 1948)
Third Base: Al Rosen (Indians, 1953)
Shortstop: Rico Petrocelli (Red Sox, 1969)
Outfield: Roger Maris (Yankees, 1961)

NL—SEASON

Pitcher: Don Drysdale (Dodgers, 1958 and 1965); Don Newcombe (Dodgers, 1955)
Catcher: Roy Campanella (Dodgers, 1953)
First Base: Johnny Mize (Giants, 1947)
Second Base: Davey Johnson (Braves, 1973)
Third Base: Eddie Matthews (Braves, 1953)
Shortstop: Ernie Banks (Cubs, 1958)
Outfield: Hack Wilson (Cubs, 1930)

AL—LIFETIME

Pitcher: Wes Ferrell (Indians)
Catcher: Yogi Berra (Yankees)
First Base: Hank Greenberg (Tigers)
Second Base: Joe Gordon (Yankees and Indians)
Third Base: Brooks Robinson (Orioles)
Shortstop: Vern Stephens (Red Sox)
Outfield: Babe Ruth (Red Sox, Yankees, and Boston Braves)

NL—LIFETIME

Pitcher: Warren Spahn (Braves)
Catcher: Roy Campanella (Dodgers)
First Base: Gil Hodges (Dodgers)
Second Base: Rogers Hornsby (Cardinals)
Third Base: Eddie Matthews (Braves)
Shortstop: Ernie Banks (Cubs)
Outfield: Willie Mays (Giants and Mets)

ANSWERS: 10. ALL-TIME TEAM HOME RUN LEADERS

1. Charles Klein
2. Hack Wilson
3. Hank Greenberg
4. Jimmy Foxx
5. Johnny Mize
6. Ralph Kiner
7. Al Rosen
8. Ted Kluszewski
9. Roger Maris
10. Frank Thomas
11. Leon Wagner
12. Frank Howard
13. Harmon Killebrew
14. Willie Mays
15. Frank Robinson
16. Jim Wynn
17. Frank Howard
18. Reggie Jackson
19. Nate Colbert
20. Tommy Harper
21. Bob Oliver
22. Rusty Staub
23. Hank Aaron (1971); Eddie Matthews (1953)
24. Rich Allen

1. Sacrifice

2. Texas leaguer

3. Spray hitter or punch hitter

4. Bunt

5. Knuckle ball

6. Pinch hitter or designated hitter

7. Hit and run

8. Gamer (RBI)

9. Bullpen

10. Hitting the dirt

11. Suicide squeeze

12. Riser

13. Submarine pitcher

14. Hot corner

15. Grand slam

16. Solo home run

17. Clutch hit

18. Error

19. Relay man or cutoff man

20. To the showers

21. Wild pitch

22. Passed ball

23. Walk

24. K

25. Run batted in (RBI)

26. Sacrifice

27. Baltimore chop

28. Force out

29. Switch hitter

30. Extra-inning game

ANSWERS: 12. BASEBALL SCORE SHEET QUIZ

A. PLAYERS NUMBERS BY FIELD POSITION

1. 9

2. 3

3. 2

4. 4

5. 7

6. 6

7. 1

8. 5

9. 8

B. SYMBOLS

1. Single

2. Error

3. Fielder's choice

4. Hit by pitch

5. Triple

6. Stolen base

7. Strike out

8. Force out

9. Base on balls

10. Sacrifice hit

11. Double

12. Passed ball

13. Balk

14. Home run

15. Wild pitch

16. Pinch hitter

C. PROBLEMS

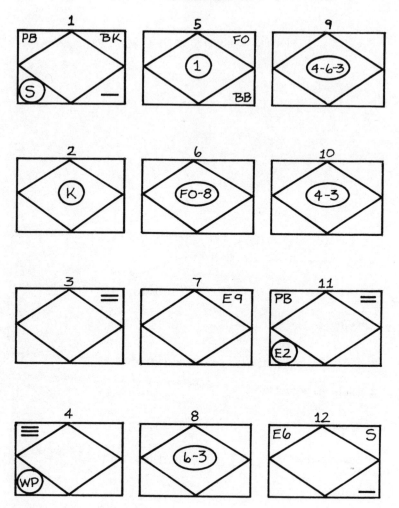

```
T C B G A Y L O R D P E R R Y R O Q Z N L W A L H O C J K E
O S F I E L M Z O E L H O A P Z O L B E N I K B L Z W X A P
L A B H O K P L H N O X P R S U M N F L Z T O A N L E O G A
H N O L Z U D O N N E W C O M B E V A N P Q P L Z T A B Z L
Z D U O H I M T B Y L Z J I M P A L M E R O K R S B R E T Z
H Y B E L M E Q R M S T L O R T C H B T U O L Z T A L C L W
I K Z V E L K U E C T W N J I M L O N B O R G I E L Y B C A
B O B G I B S O N L E O T C Y B W Z V U E Z M H V E W L Y T
P U K L E D P M Z A T E A N V K R O U V L M T L E O Y W R E
G F A V K L A B N I E O N L N K V Y I E T V U Z C R N Z R L
H A L U I T A B E N O E W K A V E L E N U G V E A K N E E P
E X A M N A T I L V D E N A T L E B V R G T I R R E O O P E
T L O U M O A L V U E L O O R V K C B E I F E G L E M V M H
A E V F H G H O M O E R G U E R P Y L O F V G H T O R E I S
M A E P S W L D O L A E T P N G E H O L A V U E O P H I J N
P E R F O R M E L M K B E O H L A N L E K U T A N E O R O I
S A N T E R C A F P O K E R U L T E S A L N L O K U N E C K
H U O L A W E N E B E E R R L O R M E P W B O K E R T E E N
O M N E L C H C O V G H I K M E O C O V A K D E L V U T T E
M O L A N N E H I O P T C U B T A C P H L H O M E G V E O J
E L A N E O R A H W L E A B C N M P O K U S N S L B C G I N
N E W S T S A N D Y K O U F A X E Z L B T W D O E C E P N O
S U N L C B P C E O L E T N M I K E M C C O R M I C K E W S
A V O N L I T E G H I M E V Z H O L E T C K Y R S L E E P U
N A C K E G F O L O T S W H O L T R A K L V S T O M A P S G
T O V U L B K P R E S I T O N T W L N O N K D E A L S P A R
A L O V A O M T W H I T E Y F O R D E S K E A R V U N T A E
C U E S U B R W H I V L B C E V H L A O N K L U C A O W E F
L O R E V A E S M O T I V A N E M I K E C U E L L A R P O V
B L O U T E R O V L I K E R U W A K O L C L U E S V U E S A
```

115

ML—1956–1966

1. 1956—Don Newcombe
2. 1957—Warren Spahn
3. 1958—Bob Turley
4. 1959—Early Wynn
5. 1960—Vernon Law
6. 1961—Whitey Ford
7. 1962—Don Drysdale
8. 1963—Sandy Koufax
9. 1964—Dean Chance
10. 1965
    1966 —Sandy Koufax

AL—1967–1973

1. 1967—Jim Lonborg
2. 1968—Denny McLain
3. 1969—Mike Cuellar
   Denny McLain (tie)
4. 1970—Jim Perry
5. 1971—Vida Blue
6. 1972—Gaylord Perry
7. 1973—Jim Palmer

NL—1967–1973

1. 1967—Mike McCormick
2. 1968—Bob Gibson
3. 1969—Tom Seaver
4. 1970—Bob Gibson
5. 1971—Ferguson Jenkins
6. 1972—Steve Carlton
7. 1973—Tom Seaver

```
A L T O O E R O I H A N K G R E E N B E R G P O V W N K O L E L O F A
O L A D E N N I S M C L A I N T L O F U R E G G I E J A C K S O N A N
M V K L P O N D E R S T R P K W N B R E A L T V D S K E V T E U R S E
L O T J E V L E F T Y G R O V E M O N Y L W O N A G E A O R E G I K Z
J O E G O R D O N E P R E T S O L V T W G O R L B C A N Q E T E A N S
Z E K L O E P R T K O M I C K E Y M A N T L E S L M N Q O S R H L A V
A B T K O Z D R E T L I K V R E N L T W N O V P U R O R M U T R E L H
C A T Z F R L I R I Q Z O T K R F A N T V L O T E B R A L O C I D O R
A T E R O G E R M A R I S T V K R L V O Q R D B C D I K T H O G S K E
R U N C K L P R T A Z K O A T R I K O M V Z R E H L T O M W V R K E C
L O A N S R O K U C G L A T E S W Q R K V E O T L T R M O E V A L K E
Y E A R Z K Q T D O A G F B R I T E R O K R C I C D K N E N S T R E R
A B K L V W N O J A C K I E J E N S E N T O W E L O C C K L A N T R E
S O O N A S Y O L K T G L O H E R O S T R D R E N O C V K A L H O E L
T O N B E A G H I F O B L K O T U V N Z E K R L A B V T S H O P S D D
R U T N S P O H O Y T K Z E L L A K S T E V A D K U S E G Q T R A I N
Z A P S T H U Q S W N K R C H A R L I E G E H R I N G E R V U R T C A
E M S K T R A N O R O T O W Q H N L K O A C D B G H L O F S O E C K H
M I T A W N Z N Q C D T E F L O K U M R E S T O V Z W R O K A C L A C
S A N K Y R L H T A U V L T O F E R H L O C D Q T A B C R E N L B L D
K A L L A N H R O Z U L O V W R E K G Q A U R O R O Z I P E O R L L U
I K O N O R E T Z S M N V U O A K T O A R E A R O L F L T Z S P E E P
B U L L O K C I T M O P E A T N K R Q T Z A W E R O Q S T V N L O N S
T A L O V E R K R T W M N O E K A B K T S Q O N R V T S L I I P A B L
O B E V T L T A B Z Q T S W N R L K G H U T H U U D S N P O B O K S T
N O W C I T U M N T S X O F N O S L E N E V N E L K U B L F O T K L A
L K C H V V L E Q C X O S E K B L E A K S T O Q U T Z O R E R E A T S
O M P L O L O E H O A X O N T I M A Z K W Q T S A B S R B H S H A E L
V V G E C C N E F F W B T O P N O A K T N O S P Z K L R O U K U C S E
K T O A K K I Y R F N M L Z K S E R V N K I L F B D C K L N O C A L L
L Q O V O I M A I L T Q E A L O M A T R N K E N R Q K E P R O L Y S E
O C B T O M C E L T Q B C R T N E A V T O V K R C K P L O E R O P E S
P K S K I O K A O U R L K G H A P U Q C A E E F R Q C K N O B R O S E
E L L J O N L H A R M O N K I L L E B R E W W S A A T S Q R O O T A S
S E T W E S K L M O N E N A R H C O C Y E K C I M E Q C B A N T A S E
```

117

1.   1931—Lefty Grove
2. 1932, 1933, 1938—Jimmy Foxx
3.   1934—Mickey Cochrane
4.   1935, 1940—Hank Greenberg
5.   1936—Lou Gehrig
6.   1937—Charlie Gehringer
7. 1939, 1941, 1947—Joe DiMaggio
8.   1942—Joe Gordon
9.   1943—Spud Chandler
10.   1944, 1945—Hal Newhouser
11.   1946, 1949—Ted Williams
12.   1948—Lou Boudreau
13.   1950—Phil Rizzuto
14. 1951, 1954, 1955—Yogi Berra
15.   1952—Bob Shantz
16.   1953—Al Rosen
17. 1956, 1957, 1962—Mickey Mantle
18.   1958—Jackie Jensen
19.   1959—Nelson Fox
20.   1960, 1961—Roger Maris
21.   1963—Elston Howard
22.   1964—Brooks Robinson
23.   1965—Zoilo Versalles
24.   1966—Frank Robinson
25.   1967—Carl Yastrzemski
26.   1968—Dennis McLain
27.   1969—Harmon Killebrew
28.   1970—Boog Powell
29.   1971—Vida Blue
30.   1972—Dick Allen
31.   1973—Reggie Jackson

ANSWERS: 15. NATIONAL LEAGUE MVP AWARD WINNERS
PUZZLE

```
A F R E I L O B C K O R Q W O R T S J E R O M E D E A N T L V O E S T
F R O K C H A R L E S K L E I N E Q W R N M O K L E A S P L H F G D E
T A L E S T P K R O K L P Q S L T R O L E H L A D B E P E T E R O S E
A N S T R O W E R O K I T V U C L U O T C R E E T E U A N B D A C K L
A K E S T O P Q E L C D R O E A C I K N L E V Q U L H O A T E N S E R
T I N O V E B M O C W E N N O D O T E L C K L M O Q S T R U C K O U V
K E N B O Y E R E L O N C A B O K B L M C O M E O N V E R N E M A A C
T F R C H L K E V Q Z W A T U R Y E S L C K C I I B O L L I N C A R E
C R E K T R O V E R N I E B A N K S E T O C L B V E S W I C K C L D E
R I T A K R A S U E T N L O N T O B E N S C O R T Q U I D H O O L T S
S S L O T P J K C I V S R H A N B T R C K R L V A R N L E Y O R T E N
K C A J K O A P T R E L O H G U Q S E R K I V R E A T L S N O M E R S
M H O V I U K O P T F J G R H O H G E C K M A U R Y W I L L S I T R Q
O D O L U M E A F T U L O L S R E U A V R E L K E B D E A R O C I O L
T E N N Y O K E R P A G R A L H O J C K O P E Z W K O M V O T K S T E
I K E R J A N O A R E A T O C K M C C L V R O K E R O A S Q U W O E R
D A P Q O L K C N D C E V R O Y C A M P A N E L L A Q Y T C A B G O H
R A L L E Y O V K S I J T L E M O N A A N E V Q S L K S E E R O K J O
A P E L M K O M R N T E A V O L A C N L T O G S E R B C L K L G O O D
B E A C E O M E O T K A L V T G B U C K Y W A L T E R S Q A L A N O T
M I T E D W L A B D L K N S O M N E T E E M Q U T G K O A T U B E A R
O T I Q W E V A I L O K S T A N M U S I A L A N T Q W R T O B T Z L
L E L K I B R A N T O E C U Y L T O E V A P E O T L O T R E A Y B H R
E D L B C A N O S K L N Q Z H D R L R O O M Q R Z O P L T R E H Z A R
I K I C K E M P O K E C B D F E C K O I E T N A W K O V E R A A T N A
N O M L Q C S A N D Y K O U F A X C I L D E T A W N P U Q A E R S K V
R A A E W L E A T H Q E Z T U G A V C E A L S K N G L H V V S T E S T
E D C V N T O N Y A V D I C K G R O A T Q O R N T U N K R A T N O A V
T E H A M D E L P H O V E V D C T K L V O N E A V T O Y Z C W E R U R
H L P L O T V G A T U L K E F R A L C O N V K H A S W X O L C T X E A
O K L E T Q O R L A N D O C E P E D A P P R C D A N X U A I Q T E R D
T B O B E L L I O T W L E B R O X W A N T S B X O V A T L H E A C K E
K O D E Q N E A K E X M O R T C O O P E R T M D B T Q C T P O T T E K
W E R K V C O O P U T R Z X Y O K A D A K T O N S M O W X V R T O E L
T M A R T Y M A R I O N B E R O E W C O O K S N O S B I G B O B N E M
```

1.		1931—Frankie Frisch
2.		1932—Charles Klein
3.	1933, 1936—	Carl Hubbell
4.		1934—Jerome Dean
5.		1935—Gabby Hartnett
6.		1937—Joe Medwick
7.		1938—Ernie Lombardi
8.		1939—Bucky Walters
9.		1940—Frank McCormick
10.		1941—Dolph Camilli
11.		1942—Mort Cooper
12.	1943, 1946, 1948—	Stan Musial
13.		1944—Marty Marion
14.		1945—Phil Cavarretta
15.		1947—Bob Elliot
16.		1949—Jackie Robinson
17.		1950—Jim Konstanty
18.	1951, 1953, 1955—	Roy Campanella
19.		1952—Hank Sauer
20.	1954, 1965—	Willie Mays
21.		1956—Don Newcombe
22.		1957—Hank Aaron
23.	1958, 1959—	Ernie Banks
24.		1960—Dick Groat
25.		1961—Frank Robinson
26.		1962—Maury Wills
27.		1963—Sandy Koufax
28.		1964—Ken Boyer
29.		1966—Roberto Clemente
30.		1967—Orlando Cepeda
31.		1968—Bob Gibson
32.		1969—Willie McCovey
33.	1970, 1972—	Johnny Bench
34.		1971—Joe Torre
35.		1973—Pete Rose

TED MISA was raised in New York City, attended Patrick Henry Junior High School and Commerce High School, then went on to a business administration degree and a financial systems and procedures degree at NYU.

Most of his free time was spent playing baseball and basketball with the Catholic Youth Organization and the Police Athletic League. He was selected for the New York City All-Star PAL and CYO baseball team.

During his stint with the U.S. Navy from 1954 to 1958, he served with both the Atlantic and Pacific Fleets and played baseball and basketball with Navy Far East and European teams, competing against other branch service teams and squads from other countries.

Mr. Misa has been an avid sports fan all his life and makes a hobby of collecting records and statistics in all sports. He still participates in softball, basketball, two-hand touch football, jogging, bowling, and baseball. A good deal of his time is spent in community activities and as a Little League umpire, basketball referee, and in helping to teach youngsters the fundamentals of baseball and basketball. He lives in Jackson, N.J., with his wife Eva and four children, Ted, Sondi, Tara, and Darren.